TRUMP'S SWAMP

THE INCOMPETENT, THE MALEVOLENT, AND THE CORRUPT

BY

KAREN ANN CARPENTER

"A MAN IS KNOWN BY THE COMPANY HE KEEPS."

— AESOP

"I SCRUTINIZE THE NEWS — SO YOU DON'T HAVE TO."

— KAREN ANN CARPENTER

"WE HAVE TO GET THE BEST PEOPLE. WE NEED TO GET THE BEST AND THE FINEST, AND IF WE DON'T, WE'LL BE IN TROUBLE FOR A LONG PERIOD OF TIME, AND MAYBE NEVER COME OUT OF IT."

— DONALD J. TRUMP

TRUMP'S SWAMP

THE INCOMPETENT, THE MALEVOLENT, AND THE CORRUPT

ISBN: 9798680383117

To the American People

God Help us all

My Fellow Americans:

I hope you enjoy reading this book and gain a few insights into the type of people currently influencing all of our futures.

I would greatly appreciate it if you left a review. Even just a few words are beneficial to the author and all potential readers.

Be sure to check out my other book about Trump:

Shameless Svengali: 101 Questions Americans Need Trump to Answer HONESTLY!

It's definitely another eye-opener.

If you like freebies (and who doesn't?) join my e-mail list. Send me an email – with **YOUR NAME,** and the word **SUBSCRIBE** in the subject to:

Karen@KarenAnnCarpenter.com

I'd love to hear from you!

THE PEOPLE DEMAND

OCTOBER, 2020

Candidate Trump promised the American people! Over and over, he vowed that if we elected him president, he would *Drain the Swamp* and *Hire Only the Best!* And what patriotic American hasn't been yearning for a fully drained swamp?

Voters kept their part of that bargain. The citizens of this exceptional nation elected Trump to the highest position in the land. Now it's Trump's turn to make right on his promise.

Unfortunately . . . we're still waiting.

After Trump took office, many Americans expected he would honor his pledge and start sucking out the scum from the boggy depths.

Instead, Trump left us sitting around, scratching our skulls, and speculating – when the heck is this guy planning on sapping those lowlands of his?

Under Trump, the Washington sinkhole has only gotten *deeper. . .* and *murkier . . .* and *scuzzier.* The swamp is so dense it's growing fur! The damned thing is smoldering and festering so feverishly – any second it might explode!

It's time for Trump to do the right thing about his obligations. We need those wastelands of his to be pristine and sparkly – exactly as he pledged.

To make draining the sinkhole easier for the man, I've assembled this list of *some* of the unsavory slinking varmints that have penetrated his domain. Though they represent only a tiny smattering of the immeasurable vermin and muddied creatures he needs to extract, if Trump starts by yanking just these bottom-feeders, he will show Americans that *finally,* he's making good on his word.

And that shouldn't be too hard. Many of the amphibious critters in this compilation have already moved on!

Not only are current bog dwellers on this list, but I've also included individuals who've previously slithered through Trump's swamp or infiltrated some of his other inner circles. The edifying information throughout this volume should drive home to Trump the type of creatures he must *never* again allow into his administration – or even into his life. *Ever*!

Our would-be monarch needs only to snap his magical fingers, wave *"bye-bye"* to the swamp dwellers contained herein and *voila*. Finally, he will be adequately on course to keeping that promise he made to the American people – *over four years ago*!

The moment is now, Trump. Americans are beyond ready to collect on your fermenting campaign promises.

START DRAINING!

AN AUTHOR'S ELUCIDATION

We all recognize that not one human being who ever existed on this planet was an unadulterated malfeasant. And we can just as easily infer that every Mother Teresa who ever lived encountered at least one inner demon, hard at work, sullying her soul.

In that vein, I don't mean to suggest that the people highlighted throughout this collection are one-dimensional. They're not necessarily just flat out, vile creatures from Trump's black lagoon. Some may be gifted and accomplished. Others might be decent, generous souls who are just stuck in their own delusional beliefs.

But the focus of this book is *draining the swamp*. Therefore, I've concentrated solely on the aspects of these swamp dwellers that illuminate why they are (or were) unfit to dwell in Trump's (*drained*) swamp!

Whether they've committed despicable deeds, or their major "crime" was being unqualified for their positions, Trump needs to put the screws to these bottom-feeders at once.

Just as there is no place for miscreants in a well-tended swamp, neither is there room for the incompetent – nor for those whom Trump invited to take the plunge through cronyism, nepotism, or because they donated big bucks to Trump World!

We can all agree that these swamp dwellers' presence does not at all depict the sanitized swamp that Trump promised us.

AN AUTHOR'S NOTES

Donald J. Trump has stocked his administration with a unique collection of The Incompetent, The Malevolent, and The Corrupt. Many of these reptiles, lizards, alligators, and snakes easily fit into *every* classification. Therefore, I didn't categorize them according to the book's title. Readers can decide for themselves if they'd like to characterize these critters any further.

Since I present this book in a quiz format, I refer to Trump's swamp dwellers as . . . well . . . as *swamp dwellers*. For the sake of the contest challenge, I could not reveal their actual names up front. That's why I used the *swamp dweller* moniker to reference the inhabitants of Trump's wastelands. Other times I might refer to them as bottom-feeders, lizards, alligators, bog dwellers, reptiles, snakes, amphibious critters, swamp creatures, muddied life forms, slinking varmints, creatures from Trump's black lagoon, or merely as dwellers. I mixed the references up to keep from overextending the *swamp dweller* term. Please consider these types of references to be interchangeable.

With all that in mind, let's get started.

READY TO HAVE SOME FUN?

I present this book in an interactive format. It's a quiz. A competition if you wish. Heck, America's swampy situation is so precarious and frightening, why not have a little diversionary fun with it?

After reading a description of each swamp dweller, I challenge readers to guess that reptile's identity. And while they're busy pondering who each person is, they should ask themselves the following questions. *If I were president or even just the head of a business, would I keep anyone of this ilk around? Would I have chosen this swamp dweller to represent me? Or hire him to reflect the ideals of my business or organization? Does she embody the best values of our country? Could I imagine myself inviting this person over for dinner? Would I trust **any** of these people alone with my kids?*

And the most relevant questions of all*: Is this Trump appointee looking out for the American people? Do I honestly think this is the type of person Trump made us believe he was referring to when he promised he would drain the swamp and hire "only the best?"*

I reveal the identities of the creatures from Trump's wasteland in the back of the book, starting on page **121**.

Though information about these muddied creatures might seem overwhelming, I only barely touched upon the wellspring of incriminatory truths about most of these snakes and lizards and alligators. These reptiles represent only a tiny sample of the many amphibious critters that inhabit Trump's wastelands. Consider this book to be more of an "introduction" to the many nefarious slinking varmints that inhabit Trump's world.

HOW TO PLAY THE TRUMP SWAMP GAME

Although the dwellers' names are not revealed up front, you can still read this compilation straight through. Whenever you're ready, just check each swamp dweller's identity in the back of the book. But why not make the experience even more interesting? Challenge yourself! Entertain yourself! Read the description of each swamp creature and see if you can guess that person's identity. After you've read each reptile's description, write down the number of that dweller and your guess as to his or her identity.

When you've finished, check the answers in the back of the book, starting on page **121**. Just match up the numbers with the original numbers in each person's description.

I have listed the answers five to a page and spaced them out to keep readers from inadvertently spotting upcoming swamp dwellers' identities.

Tally your number of correct answers. Award yourself four points for each accurate guess. After you've completed chapter five, your test score can be up to 100.

But wait . . . if your score isn't where you'd hoped it might be, there's a chance to redeem yourself . . . big time! I've included a bonus round. In this brief chapter six, you'll find just two dwellers. But you can slap yourself on the back and award yourself *ten* additional points for each correct guess in this extra credit bonus round! The perfect chance to play catch up!

Overall, a perfect score would be 120!

Once you've totaled your correct answers, check to see what your score reveals about you. You can find this directly after the answers. Are you "in the know" or do you have a lot to learn?

Play *Trump's Swamp Game* with your family and friends. Read the book out loud at parties or online. Have everyone write down their guesses and see who has the highest score at the end. Or get creative – allow people to call out their answers before you reveal all the clues. Award them extra credit if they guess correctly early on. Maybe even take a few points away if they guess wrong? You can easily tailor this game for any gathering.

You could also take the test on your own, then later compare scores with your friends. Find out who in your crowd is really "in the know." Who amongst you is most informed about these countless swampy creatures that are controlling our fine country and all of our futures?

And guess what? Even if your responses prove you *had* a lot to learn, after reading this book, you too will be "in the know!"

As Trump likes to say: "What have you got to lose?"

Ready to get muddy? Put on your clunkiest waterproof boots, and let's head on down to Trump's wetlands. It's time to meet some of his most audacious amphibious creatures.

CONTENTS

CHAPTER ONE ~

CROOKED CABINET

Many historians believe that Donald Trump (*the self-proclaimed drainer of the swamp*) has put together the most corrupt cabinet in the United States' history. Following are just a few of his choices:

SWAMP DWELLER NUMBER ONE

- This dweller's family runs Foremost, a prominent American shipping company based in China. For an American business, Foremost does a lot of collaborating with the Chinese regime. When this swamp dweller was labor secretary under George W. Bush, she gave her father (who ran the company until recently) unfettered access to China's Premier. She let her father sit in on private government sessions.

- Leading up to her initial trip to China as a representative of Trump's bog, she requested to include several relatives in official government meetings. She even had the audacity to ask federal administrators to arrange travel for a family member.

- These requests stirred up ethics questions with American government officials. After several news outlets dug into her proposed itinerary, she abruptly canceled the *entire* trip.

- This swamp creature has regularly sought to bolster her family's company's profile by using her government position and influences. She's appeared at Foremost promotional events and joined in Chinese media interviews with her father.

- Though this resident of Trump's sinkhole has no official ownership in the shipping firm, she and her spouse have received millions in benefits and campaign contributions from family members connected to the business.

- This shipping business is a company that has received loan commitments in the hundreds of millions of greenbacks from a

Chinese national bank. Trump's administration has classified the policies of this bank as a threat to America's security.

- While her family's company in China prospers, this bottom-feeder and her husband continue to be beneficiaries of its good fortune.

- In spite of, or *because of* this woman's glaring conflicts, Trump chose this swampy organism to be the principal official overseeing the *American shipping* industry.

- In her position, this muddied creature has continually requested to cut programs designed to sustain America's maritime industry.

- Congress has rejected these cuts – for now at least – but the swamp resident keeps proposing them.

- Representative Alan Lowenthal said, "The Chinese government is massively engaged in maritime expansion as we have walked away from it. There is going to come a crisis, and we are going to call upon the U.S. maritime industry, and it is not going to be around."

- Guess who this dweller's spouse is? Come on, you know . . . the guy who helps this reptile spend all that spillover money from her family's shipping enterprise. He's none other than Senate Majority Leader Mitch McConnell! *Moscow Mitch*, the man with the perfect track record for protecting Trump! This dude blocks everything from even being discussed on the Senate floor that he suspects might not be in Trump's *personal* interests.

- This critter signed an ethics agreement when she first slithered into Trump's swamp. She agreed to cash out her stock options in one of the nation's largest highway construction materials suppliers. Owning these stocks is another obvious conflict of interest in her position as the United States secretary of transportation. She just never considered it necessary to follow through on her promises.

- This reptile also funnels huge grant monies to her husband's home state of Kentucky, as he prepares to run for re-election.

SWAMP DWELLER NUMBER TWO

- This dweller had never set foot inside a public school before joining Trump's swamp. Neither had any of her four children.

- This reptile even went on record to proclaim she'd always thought public schools were "dead ends."

- Despite that, or *because of* it, Trump nominated her to be in charge of all the public schools in America.

- Word has it when Trump signed her nominating papers, he looked at her, said her name, then proclaimed: "Education. *Right?*"

- This dweller was such a controversial candidate Mike Pence had to break the Senate tie at her confirmation hearing. This was the first time in U.S. history a vice president had to be called in to confirm a Cabinet nominee.

- Although she and her family members generously donated to the private college she had attended, at least 2,700 students and alumni from that college presented an open letter protesting her nomination.

- During her confirmation hearing, this bog dweller fumbled through countless questions. On one issue, she submitted a 62-page reply, much of which she'd lifted directly from other sources.

- She couldn't even show that she understood the Individuals with Disabilities in Education Act.

- This alligator has worked to take money out of the public schools and put it into charter schools, which has had devastating consequences on our country's public schools.

- According to statistics, the education children receive from charter schools is often inferior to the education they could have received in public schools.

- This swamp dweller has also tirelessly fought to deregulate charter schools. These types of actions further degrade the quality of education in these money-grabbing institutions.

- This reptile believes that all schools should be religious in nature and wants to inflict her personal beliefs on all of our children.

- At a Christian meeting, she professed that education reform was a way to "advance God's Kingdom." While charter schools cannot legally affiliate themselves with a religion, they have invented many ways to easily get around that. It's incredibly easy for them now since this dweller has fought so hard to deregulate these schools.

- At a gathering of America's wealthiest Christians, this alligator explained why she is an animating force behind education reform: "It goes back to what I mentioned, the concept of really being active in the Shephelah of our culture – to impact our culture in ways that are not the traditional, funding-the-Christian-organization route, but that really may have greater Kingdom gain in the long run by changing the way we approach things – in this case, the system of education in the country."

- *Kingdom* gain? What ever happened to providing students with a quality education?

- The alligator's husband added: "The church – which ought to be, in our view, far more central to the life of the community – has been displaced by the public school. We just can think of no better way to rebuild our families and our communities than to have that circle of church and school and family much more tightly focused and built on a consistent worldview."

- *World* view?

- The dweller's "highly religious" brother is the founder of the government military services company, Blackwater USA. Blackwater's employees fired their weapons into a crowd of Iraqi civilians and massacred seventeen innocent people.

- Two former employees testified in federal court that they believed the Blackwater founder "views himself as a Christian crusader."

- The dweller's brother also recruited ex-spies to infiltrate liberal groups.

- The combined net worth of the dweller's family is estimated to be well over $5 *billion*. Their combined donations to Republican causes and political campaigns surpassed $100 million!

- This dweller's husband's family business made a fortune using what many believed to be a pyramid scheme. The Federal Trade Commission did a six-year investigation into the company but came up short of establishing an iron-clad case against the family.

- The Canadian government filed criminal charges against the company, alleging they had defrauded the country out of $28 million in customs duties and then forged receipts to cover its tracks. This time, members of the company pled guilty to fraud.

- This company cut many of its American jobs and shipped them to China. A definite violation of Trump's so-called *Made in America* policy.

- This bottom-feeder (a billionaire heiress) and her family set up *250* dark shell corporations to hide their wealth.

- This alligator and her family's investments raise conflicts of interest with her position in Trump's bog, especially since she and her family have made millions from student loan refinancing.

- The dweller's family also has had investments in a controversial for-profit charter school company.

- When someone vandalized this dweller's $40 million yacht (one of the family's ten such luxury toys), people noticed that her boat was flying the Cayman Islands flag.

- With the yacht registered in another country, this swamp creature has avoided regulations, taxes, domestic employment laws, and any need for transparency.

- After a vandal set her yacht adrift, Ohio taxpayers had to fork over the money to retrieve it. At the same time, this reptile saved approximately $2.4 million by not proudly waving America's stars and stripes.

- As an official in Trump's swamp, she proposed cutting student loan relief by $13 billion. This money was intended for students who had been defrauded by for-profit colleges. The dweller is heavily invested in one such college

- As a partner in Trump's wetlands, she also announced that she was reversing the Obama-era limits on fees that Americans pay for defaulting on their federal student loans.

- Because of this decision, one company – United Student Aid Funds Inc. – will probably earn an additional $15 million per year. Coincidentally, the father of one of this swamp dweller's aides (who conveniently resigned after the dweller's announcement) led this organization.

- For-profit colleges take advantage of a federal loophole and make fortunes from taxpayer support of veterans who often end up with garbage degrees. Nearly two dozen state attorneys general have warned that within five years, the government will waste $2.3 billion on improper payments to these institutions.

- Many of the for-profit schools receiving G.I. bill subsidies have faced legal action by the government for defrauding students.

- This swamp dweller has the power to undercut this fraud but has instead designated the policymaking and enforcement to members *of the for-profit-college industry* – allowing them to regulate *themselves*. She even hired many of these unsavory people as her aides.

- One of her aides' organizations just settled to the tune of half a billion dollars for defrauding students.

- One of this alligator's top deputies also worked for that organization, as well as at another for-profit college organization that is facing numerous government investigations.

- This dweller also hired someone to run her enforcement unit who then buried numerous ongoing investigations focusing on his former employer and other large for-profit colleges. When the scandal broke, the dweller merely shifted this hire to another position.

- This reptile gathered a panel in Washington (most of them representing for-profit colleges) to push proposals to weaken many additional regulations that govern the quality of these colleges.

- The inspector general of this swamp dweller's own department investigated her at the urging of the Veteran's Administration.

- This amphibious creature reinstated the Accrediting Council for Independent Colleges and Schools (ACICS) even after career civil servants had determined that this organization had failed to meet nearly two-thirds of basic federal quality standards. One of this dweller's senior aides even produced phony letters of support for ACICS!

- She also pitched a $5 billion federal tax credit to fund scholarships to private schools.

- The late Elijah Cummings prompted an internal investigation into this dweller's e-mails, claiming that she used her private email account at least 100 times while conducting official business. She did not archive any of those communications.

- This swamp creature strongly supports using biofeedback technology to help kids enhance their school performance. Along with her husband, she is one of the most prominent financial investors in Neurocore, a company that operates "brain performance centers."

- In an agreement with the Office of Government Ethics, this dweller claimed that she had stepped down from the Neurocore board. But she refused to surrender her financial interest in this goldmine – which she valued at between $5 million and $25 million in her financial disclosure statement.

- She had previously told lawmakers that she would divest of her business interests in 102 other companies. Ethical entanglements continue to emerge on many of these.

- She rolled back Obama-era policies that provided guidelines to protect sexual assault victims on college campuses.

- Though the swamp put this dweller in charge of a federal school safety commission (created in the aftermath of the Parkland Florida school shooting), she said that the commission would *not* be looking into the role guns play in school violence.

- This airhead reptile backed Trump when he pulled out of the Paris climate accord. A few days later, when reporters questioned her on those views, she conceded: "Certainly, the climate changes . . . Yes."

- When this dweller appeared on *60 Minutes*, her primary "defense" of her school policies was: "I hesitate to talk about all schools in general because schools are made up of individual students attending them." She admitted that she had never "intentionally" visited a low-performing traditional public school.

- An internal memo obtained by *The New York Times* showed that this swamp creature's department scaled back on investigations of civil rights violations at public schools and colleges.

- The dweller wouldn't even say whether the federal government should prevent private schools from discriminating against students, even when those schools accept public money.

- There have been multiple lawsuits about this varmint's handling of the Borrower Defense to Repayment program. A federal judge held this dweller in contempt of court for continuing (after being ordered to stop) to illegally intercept federal refunds and seize wages from student borrowers who had been defrauded by for-profit educational institutions.

- This dweller has also tirelessly campaigned to weaken labor unions.

SWAMP DWELLER NUMBER THREE

- This amphibious creature had zero experience or training for the position that Trump granted him.

- This reptile's aide explained that this snake would have to turn down any Trump administration position because of his lack of experience. "The last thing he would want to do was take a position that could cripple the presidency," the aide insisted.

- This swampy creature himself informed us he was unqualified. "Having me as a federal bureaucrat would be like a fish out of water, quite frankly," he said.

- The dweller also told us that as a teenager, he would "go after people with rocks, and bricks, and baseball bats, and hammers."

- He claims he once attacked a schoolmate with a combination lock.

- The dweller added: "And, of course, many people know the story when I was fourteen, and I tried to stab someone."

- The snake claimed the only reason he didn't go through with the slashing was that his blade broke in his friend's belt buckle. Potentially, the dweller could have murdered his buddy – and all because the friend had changed the radio station.

- After arguing over clothing, he tried to bash his own mother's brains in with a hammer.

- The snake claims he completely cured his anger issues by reading from the Book of Proverbs.

- The reptile repeatedly told of these past events in his books and public speeches.

- After a CNN investigation failed to uncover proof of some of these incidents, this reptile posted an old news article on Facebook, where his mother verified the stabbing incident.

- This muddied creature credited a company's nutritional supplements with curing his prostate cancer symptoms while giving paid speeches at that company's events and promoting their products.

- He continued his affiliation with this company even after the courts forced them to pay $7 million in a deceptive marketing lawsuit.

- Despite this dweller's dubious past and total lack of experience for any government position, or maybe *because of* all that, Trump welcomed him into the swamp.

- The dweller's business manager stated that this reptile: " . . . was never offered a specific position, but *everything* was open to him."

- Soon after taking up a position in Trump's swamp, this bog dweller ordered a $31,000 dining set for his office.

- He claimed he wasn't involved in the purchase, but emails that were later uncovered revealed that wasn't true.

- A career government employee filed a complaint alleging that Trump's swamp bosses demoted her, then fired her, shortly after she refused to exceed the $5,000 legal limit on the redecoration of agency offices for this dweller.

- While testifying before Congress about the purchase, the reptile threw his wife under the bus, stating that she had ordered the furniture. Again, emails proved the dweller's personal involvement.

- He also spent over $8,000 installing a dishwasher in his office kitchen. Any such expenditures over $5,000 needed to be reported to Congress, but he did not provide any advance notice.

- This slinking varmint allowed his son, a private citizen, to organize and participate in a "listening tour" of governmental agency meetings.

- The dweller's son invited other outside people, then put those invitees in touch with his father's deputies.

- The invitees joined in on governmental conference calls along with this snake's son.

- According to the department's deputy general counsel for operations, they had concerns that this gave the appearance that the dweller might be using his position for his son's private gain.

- The dweller's wife and daughter-in-law also attended official governmental meetings, causing the department's inspector general's office to investigate.

- This swamp creature often appears ill-informed. During congressional testimony, he confused the term R-E-O (Real Estate Owned) with the Oreo cookie.

- He believes that the Baltic states should "get involved in NATO." They are NATO *members*.

- Many of the top political jobs in this dweller's agency remain vacant.

- In his position, supposedly as an advocate for people who live in public housing, he rolled back efforts to enforce the fair housing policy.

- After securing his position in Trump's bog, this dweller suddenly began claiming that he DOES have enough experience for the job – because he grew up in the projects.

- The dweller, who has clearly forgotten where he came from, proposed tripling rents for public housing's most impoverished tenants.

<u>SWAMP DWELLER NUMBER FOUR</u>

- This dweller is a Wall Street guy, a billionaire hedge fund manager who worked at Goldman Sachs. *Precisely the type of person (totally disconnected from the average Joe), that Trump promised us he'd be draining.*

- This dweller also served as the chairman of OneWest, the corporate parent of a bank called Financial Freedom.

- The California attorney general's office found evidence of "widespread misconduct" at OneWest.

- The dweller's bank obstructed the attorney general's investigation by ordering third parties not to comply with subpoenas.

- Many parties have testified that OneWest engaged in cruel, shoddy, and deceptive banking practices.

- The bank has been accused of racial redlining, with extreme disparities in lending to minority communities.

- Under this muddied creature, the bank allegedly foreclosed on a 90-year-old woman because her mortgage payment was short by 27 cents.

- The bank is said to have locked out another homeowner during a blizzard.

- Another customer testified that this bank, under this alligator's management, "encouraged" her father, while he was terminally ill and heavily medicated, to sign for a reverse mortgage that he clearly didn't need. She also testified that after her father died, the bank moved to foreclose on the property, although her family offered to repay the loan in full. Subsequently, this woman fought for over a decade to prevent the bank from foreclosing on her family's home.

- A former OneWest Bank vice president admitted that the institution's employees robo-signed approximately *six thousand* foreclosure-related documents every *week*. More often than not, the employees never read the documents they signed.

- Under this reptile's "watchful eye," the bank engaged in dual tracking, which means they pretended to be helping homeowners modify their mortgages while all the while they were moving to foreclose on their properties.

- OneWest has also been cited for backdating documents, which can speed up the foreclosure process. They fraudulently backdated some of those documents to dates before the bank even existed.

- This alligator's bank became known as the "foreclosure machine."

- Financial Freedom had to pay more than $89 million to the U.S. Department of Housing and Urban Development (HUD) after its investigation into the bank revealed it violated the False Claims Act and the Financial Institutions Reform, Recovery and Enforcement Act.

- This dweller's company agreed to make this payment to close a governmental investigation into its practice of allegedly not conforming to HUD's requirements.

- The dweller eventually sold OneWest for $3.5 billion. Due to his being a primary actor in America's foreclosure crisis (by having preyed upon struggling homeowners during the recession), many say this creature from Trump's black lagoon pocketed more than $200 million from the sale.

- This dweller made millions off the backs of vulnerable people during his time at OneWest. He even departed the bank with a severance of nearly $11 million.

- During his tenure at the bank, he frequently shifted American jobs to Mumbai and Bangalore. *America first?*

- CIT Bank, where this dweller was deputy chairman, provided customers with financing structures in the tens of millions of dollars, which helped customers avoid paying sales tax.

- This reptile's bank was under a consent decree by the Treasury Department just two years before Trump nominated him to be the head of that same department.

- Although this alligator has consistently proven to be ruthless and cruel, and an incompetent, corrupt banker who had zero governmental experience – *or maybe because of these qualities* – Trump granted this dweller oversight over every national bank in the country!

- Trump chose this scoundrel to be the face of the U.S. economy. He charged him with collecting our taxes, managing the nation's debt, enforcing federal finance laws, consigning our currency, overseeing banking regulations, etc., etc.

- This swamp creature had a $1million to $2 million investment in a hedge fund, which betted on the privatization of Fannie Mae and Freddie Mac. Before being confirmed, this dweller had committed to advancing that privatization.

- Once in his new position in the swamp, this dweller intervened with governmental guidelines to help his buddy, Michael Milken. This 1980's junk bond king had been convicted of securities fraud and served several years in prison.

- The reptile described this criminal as "beyond remarkable."

- The alligator's maneuvering helped to boost the value of Milken's property through a program originally meant to help distressed communities.

- While in Trump's swamp, this dweller used military aircraft for many of his brief trips, costing taxpayers over $800,000 in 2017 alone.

- The bottom-feeder also inquired about using military aircraft for his honeymoon.

- This dweller, a former filmmaker, helped produce the 2017 film "Wonder Woman." The movie made big bucks in China, but due to the country's strict foreign film laws, the American filmmakers only cashed in on a small portion of that windfall.

- In his position in Trump's swamp, this muddied creature has pushed to change those specific laws in China, which would prove lucrative to the dweller's *former* industry.

- But has the dweller honestly put the Hollywood glitz and glamour behind him? After all, he did marry an actress and filmmaker.

- This reptile claimed to have divested from his film production company when he plunged headfirst into the murky depths. But who the heck do you think "bought him out?"

- The dweller's wife, who else?

SWAMP DWELLER NUMBER FIVE

- Trump claimed he wanted to drain the swamp of the super-rich and fill his administration with people more in touch with average Americans. Perhaps Trump didn't realize this dweller owns a mansion in Washington, D.C., another in the Berkshires, and two more multimillion-dollar properties in Palm Beach?

- This swamp creature also owns an art collection valued at $150 million.

- Back in the day, this dweller brokered a deal for Trump that enabled Trump to re-capitalize his failing casinos. *Perhaps that helped get this dweller into his current day position?*

- This snake learned that the wealthier he appeared, the more readily people invested in his ventures. Even with all his riches, he has significantly exaggerated his net worth on many occasions just to assure a prime spot on the *Forbes* list of the wealthiest Americans.

- This dweller uses offshore havens to avoid paying his fair share of taxes.

- Before being appointed to the swamp, this reptile made a fortune by acquiring failed companies and selling them for huge profits. He became known as the "King of Bankruptcy."

- At least ten of this dweller's former employees claimed that this snake had a penchant for misleading colleagues and investors.

- The dweller's dishonesty resulted in him being forced to refund tens of millions of dollars to the victims of his schemes.

- One colleague, who worked with this swampy creature for 25 years, observed that this inhabitant of Trump's bog "doesn't have an issue with bending the truth."

- Another colleague claimed outright: "He's lied to a lot of people."

- One former employee claimed this dweller's firm sent him inaccurate financial information and that the dweller stole his interests outright.

- A vice-chairman of the dweller's firm claimed that the snake tried to cut him out of promised fees and interest.

- A member of the European Parliament accused this reptile of insider trading from a 2014 sale of shares in the Bank of Ireland.

- This varmint reimbursed investors $11.8 million and paid a fine of $2.3 million to settle a probe by the U.S. Securities and Exchange Commission into his organization's overcharging of fees. The dweller never admitted liability, though five former employees and investors claimed the reptile's firm charged investors fees on money it had lost, including on a worthless investment.

- Even though this dweller is a significant player in the auto parts industry, or possibly *because of* the conflict, Trump granted this dweller a position that provided him a say in trade policy decisions.

- Trump issued a statement saying that he'd instructed this muddied creature to start an investigation into imports of automobiles and automobile parts, supposedly to determine whether the United States should impose new taxes on foreign cars and parts. The outcome of the investigation could potentially make the dweller much more affluent than he already is.

- Before this reptile plunged into the Trump sinkhole, he signed an ethics form attesting to the divestiture of certain assets. That attestation was false.

- During his Senate confirmation hearing, the dweller agreed to sell his stocks before the end of May 2017. After it became known the dweller was still earning millions from stock that he'd promised to divest, this creature claimed that he mistakenly believed that he had sold all his previously held stock.

- Only after the government's top ethics watchdog warned of a potential for a "serious criminal violation" did this critter announce he would *actually* sell the rest of his stock.

- The dweller may have eventually divested himself of many of his assets, but he actually only passed them off to a family trust; all of his conflicts of interest remain.

- This dweller had joint assets with a Chinese-government-owned entity.

- He also had a stake in a shipping company owned partly by Russian oligarchs, cronies of Vladimir Putin, which he failed to disclose during his confirmation hearing.

- The reptile also failed to disclose a lawsuit from his ex-business partner. The dweller settled that suit after being subpoenaed, apparently suppressing information he did not want to be revealed.

- According to six U.S. senators, this snake initially failed to mention at least 19 lawsuits when he responded to a questionnaire during his confirmation process.

- While trying to pull several fast ones during his confirmation, he blatantly lied, declaring: "I intend to be quite scrupulous about recusal and any topic where there is the slightest scintilla of doubt."

- While in office, the dweller also maintained partial ownership of a Cypriot bank that was part of Mueller's investigation.

- After journalists questioned this bog dweller about his connections to a firm, but before their reports became public, this reptile bet against that company's stock. Using insider information to make money in stock trades is illegal. The dweller denied having done so.

- Though the dweller's wife owned a substantial investment in Chevron, this dweller met with their executives in his official capacity in the swamp.

- He also met with the CEO of Boeing, even though his wife also owns a stake in that company.

- In 2019, the United States Office of Government Ethics rejected this dweller's financial disclosure.

- In 2017, this reptile went with Trump on his first foreign visit to Saudi Arabia. The snake bragged about the tour being a colossal success since none of the locals protested against the Trump swamp. Was he not even aware that Saudi Arabia has long-since banned demonstrations and protests?

- During the federal government shutdown, this dweller stated that he could not believe that unpaid government employees had to visit a food bank. He suggested they instead take out personal loans to feed their families.

- Career employees have reported significant dysfunction in the department that this dweller heads. Sources say the workers see this reptile as irrelevant, and the morale in his department is abysmal. Allegedly this dweller has spent so much time trying to woo Trump's approval that he left his department leaderless.

- This snake has used private email to conduct government business. *Lock him up! Lock him up!*

- The word is that this dweller falls asleep during critical meetings, including during Trump's address to the United Nations General Assembly. Senior staffers have had to avoid putting him into some of the more critical meetings for that reason.

- The dweller even nodded off during a presentation meant to ready the country for any potential pandemics.

- On the coronavirus, he commented: "I think it will help to accelerate the return of jobs to North America."

- A federal judge ruled that this snake broke the law when he misled the public about his department's attempt to add a 2020 census question. He intended for the issue to frighten Latinos and keep them from replying to the poll so that immigrant-heavy communities would be undercounted and underfunded. This dweller tried to convince people that the question was there to protect the rights of African American voters.

- After Trump blundered by spreading an inaccurate hurricane prediction, this dweller threatened to fire officials at the National Oceanic and Atmospheric Administration (NOAA) for doing their job and providing an accurate forecast.

- This muddied creature cut short his travels in order to "encourage" NOAA officials to put out a false statement that would make Trump look good.

- The agency did eventually issue such a statement, but no one dared sign it.

- A former ex-colleague of this reptile had this to say about Trump's swamp dweller: "Everybody does *some* cheating, everybody does *some* lying. Not everybody steals from their employees."

CHAPTER TWO –

HERE COME DA DRUNKS

Trump swears his lips have never touched alcohol. This one claim of his (though likely hyperbolic) *might* actually be close to the truth. We've seen pictures of him raising symbolic toasts at key events – but could he have been drinking his signature Diet Coke? A handful of people from Trump's wild party days insist that Trump regularly imbibed back then. Is it possible they were . . . *mistaken*?

Mostly, as reports and rumors swirl, the word is that Trump actually doesn't drink. At least not these days. People close to him have claimed that he's vehemently opposed to alcohol and disapproves when others indulge. In 2015, while on MSNBC's Morning Joe, Trump stated: "I've seen people that have very smart children. When they go bad on drugs or alcohol – and I add cigarettes in there – but when they go bad, these kids are wiped out. Doesn't matter how smart. The world is so competitive that you can't lose that extra percentage."

Makes you wonder . . .

Why, then, has Trump let so many drunks get a powerful foothold inside the White House? The *People's* House? *Our* House. Why would he nominate a man (who has crossed that drunken threshold far too many times) to the Supreme Court?

While we're asking ourselves these questions, we might also wonder: If Trump is so steadfast in his abhorrence of alcohol, why would he promote Trump Vodka? And why does he own a winery?

The answer is the same as it always has been, still is, and always will be with Trump's dichotomies. This man will do anything and *everything* – if he thinks it will benefit him.

As far as allowing drunks into his administration – as long as someone is loyal to the death to the perceived king, Trump doesn't give a damn if that person reports to work crawling and slithering across the White House floor. He can burn holes in the wood flooring with his lethal alcohol breath while mouthing obscenities and incoherent plans for America – just so long as the press doesn't get wind of any scandals. Or the FBI doesn't raid the drunk's home and office and vault and uncover proof of more of Trump's dirty deeds. That would force Trump to feign shock and disgust and say he hardly knew the guy – he was just *another* coffee boy. Then he'd have to roll that drunken, hapless soul under the bus – with all the others that Trump has thrown under there before him. Later he'd pardon the bum if he feared he might talk.

In this chapter, we'll examine some of the people in Trump's circle who are known to have had, or at least *appear* to have had, their fair share of "experience" with alcohol.

<u>SWAMP DWELLER NUMBER SIX</u>

- Among various other governmental positions, this dweller once served as U.S. Attorney for the Southern District of New York. While there, he had a successful record of prosecuting corruption in government and putting away drug dealers.

- He also went after "the mob," indicting many organized crime figures, including the heads of the "Five Families." Some say members of the mob had a hit out on this dweller's life.

- Later in this snake's career, as Mayor of New York City, many people credited him with lowering crime and improving the quality of life. He became a prominent figure throughout the world when he took command of the city after the September 11th attacks.

- But even back then, *his true Trumpian nature* seeped through the cracks in his armor. Many claimed that New York's crime rates were already on the decline in the city, and this dweller's brutal use of racial profiling only hurt New York's citizens without helping in the fight against crime.

- This snake also hired people who weren't qualified for their positions. Several of the people he appointed to head city agencies became the subject of criminal proceedings.

- He often ignored his advisers. Experts surmise that we lost people unnecessarily on September 11th because of this dweller's inadequate planning.

- He ignored the recommendations of his team and the New York City Police Department when they advised him NOT to place the Office of Emergency Management at the World Trade Center, an area considered a prime target for terrorists.

- And, just like Trump, this dweller doesn't mind throwing others under the bus when fighting to salvage his own reputation. After the Emergency Management office was rendered useless and destroyed on September 11th, this snake blamed a team member for its placement. Evidence suggests this claim was false.

- This reptile also did not provide adequate radios for his New York City Fire Department. On September 11th, once the fire chiefs realized the towers were doomed to collapse, they ordered their emergency personnel out of the buildings. At least 343 firefighters likely perished because their radios weren't working; they never heard their chief's commands.

- Trump's future bottom-feeder had the gall to declare that *all* 343 of those firefighters deliberately disobeyed their evacuation orders and stayed behind in a collapsing building because they wanted to save more lives!

- This dweller seized control of the September 11th cleanup from the usual Federal agencies. He quickly reopened Wall Street and claimed that the air quality was "safe and acceptable." According to documents, he did not enforce the federal requirement that rescue and cleanup crews wear respirators. He even threatened to dismiss companies working at the Ground Zero site if their work slowed down.

- Christine Todd Whitman, the Director of the Environmental Protection Agency at the time, stated that she had pushed for the cleanup workers to wear respirators, but this reptile blocked the action. Though Oprah Winfrey had once dubbed this dweller to be "America's Mayor," many believe that he is responsible for the subsequent cases of lung disease and deaths suffered by numerous first responders.

- The dweller denied those allegations and even asked a congressional delegation to limit the city's liability for illnesses suffered by the workers in the aftermath of the collapse of the Twin Towers.

- The International Association of Fire Fighters claimed this reptile rushed to shut down cleanup operations just after they recovered the silver and gold from the vaults beneath the World Trade Center's rubble.

- They stated that this dweller's actions " . . . meant that firefighters and citizens who perished would either remain buried at Ground Zero forever, with no closure for families, or be removed like garbage and deposited at the Fresh Kills Landfill." A federal legal action alleges that New York City negligently dumped body parts and other human remains in that landfill.

- This snake has divorced several wives and has a history of being unfaithful to his spouses.

- Rumors have swirled for some time that this dweller has a drinking problem. Supposedly, Trump's old buddy expected Trump would give him a prominent position in the Washington swamp, but Trump refused to do so because of the dweller's drinking issues. Further, Trump allegedly claimed that this dweller falls asleep five minutes into meetings.

- And yet – Trump didn't mind hiring this drunkard as his personal attorney. Nor did he object to delegating America's foreign policy on Ukraine to the guy who not only seems incapable of staying awake at meetings but continues to make a fool of himself on national television.

- The dweller's close associates have stated that he hangs out at a cigar bar and has gotten buzzed just before television interviews.

- During one TV appearance, he heatedly denied that he'd asked the Ukrainian government to investigate Vice President Joe Biden's son, Hunter Biden. Seconds later, in response to the same question, he shouted: "Of course I did!"

- Throughout a series of increasingly unhinged interviews, television hosts even commented on-air about this dweller's inebriation. One gave him the moniker "Drunk Grandpa."

- According to White House sources, Trump's allies recommended Trump ban this swampy organism from TV appearances; they too believed he was getting sloshed just before interviews.

- Until the time comes when Trump absolutely *must* throw this dweller under the bus, Trump stands by his man.

- Could that be because this dweller has alluded to having some sort of *protective insurance* stashed away somewhere?

- Several news outlets have claimed this dweller is under investigation by the Southern District of New York, the organization that he once led.

- He's being investigated for violating lobby laws linked to his pursuits in Ukraine. It's likely the investigations could extend to conspiracy, bribery of foreign officials, and suspicion of a profit motive with his interest in a Ukrainian natural gas endeavor.

- Numerous other charges are also possible on the horizon, such as making false statements to the federal government, mail/wire fraud, conspiracy to defraud the United States, obstruction of justice, and money laundering.

- Trump's stooge, Attorney General William Barr, is clearly trying his damnedest to make the charges against this dweller go away.

- The reptile denies all charges (even the one of overindulging) but admits he likes to "drink with cigars."

- *"I am not guilty. I am beautiful,"* or so this reptile claims.

- According to this dweller, he worked as an adviser for Trump for over four years, though people in Trump World mostly try to distance themselves from the man.

- Trump's campaign fired the dweller after his racially charged Facebook posts hit the presses. It's rare for Trump to give a damn about stuff like that. For a moment, it appeared as if Trump might actually be making at least a limited attempt to drain his sinkhole.

- But does anyone honestly believe that Trump was *appalled* and *offended* when learning this dweller called Barack Obama a "Socialist Marxist Islamo Fascist Nazi Appeaser"?

- Trump wanted this bottom-feeder out because the guy broke Trump's two cardinal rules: 1) *Whatever happens in the swamp, stays in the swamp!* 2) *Never criticize the king. Or his kingdom.* ***EVER!***

- How convenient for Trump to get rid of the guy while also pretending his campaign had a few scruples.

- Trump ended up filing a $10 million lawsuit against this dweller, alleging that he'd violated a confidentiality agreement.

- During Trump's election campaign, this dweller helped formulate the phony promise of building a wall – and having Mexico pay for it.

- Not only has Mexico not paid for the wall, but as of October 2020, there have only been *five miles* of new fence built, though Trump keeps bragging otherwise.

- This alligator worked closely with Roger Stone, another loony from Trump's swamp. A jury found Stone guilty on five counts of lying to Congress, one count of witness tampering, and one count of obstruction of a proceeding.

- This dweller's public drunken meltdown began when he got a subpoena to testify in Special Counsel Robert Mueller's investigation. On live television, he repeatedly ranted that he would not comply with the subpoena.

- He fumed about having to pay his own legal fees (*a hint maybe for Trump to pay them if he kept his mouth shut about stuff?*)

- He raged about being compelled to uncover old emails that Mueller had requested.

- This alligator got so charged up on live television, he even dared Mueller to arrest him!

- The dweller also speculated about Trump's alleged crimes.

- He denounced Corey Lewandowski.

- He blurted out his observation that Sarah Huckabee Sanders was a "fat slob."

- Throughout his meltdown though, he still swore allegiance to his mentor and father figure, the almighty Roger Stone!

- This reptile sounded off on-air to at least three CNN reporters and two MSNBC reporters. He made appearances on Bloomberg TV and Spectrum News NY1. He also raved to several other news organizations, including *Politico* and *The Washington Post*.

- Clara Jeffery, an editor at *Mother Jones,* asked: "What are the networks' policies about allowing someone who might be drunk or on a manic binge to keep going on air?" Scott Simon from NPR added, "I'm not a professional, but I'm not sure he's all right."

- White House officials called into the networks stating that this reptile's interviews were "bizarre" and "nuts." A Trump ally exclaimed that this dweller was "drunk or off his meds."

- Erin Burnett of CNN confronted the muddied creature: "Talking to you, I have smelled alcohol on your breath."

- The dweller denied drinking. When asked if he'd taken anything else, he replied: "Antidepressants, is that OK?" After Burnett informed this dweller that Trump's team had been calling in to the network, the dweller replied: "They can say whatever they want, they are pathetic … I didn't steal from the campaign; I didn't have an illicit affair with a married man. All I did was work with him for four and a half years, and now I get this crap."

- Remember, this dweller is not guilty of anything. *He's beautiful!*

- If you spend any time at all on social media, you saw the video that nearly broke the Internet! The quick clip showed a male actor chatting it up with Trump and Melania at the College Football Playoff Championship in New Orleans. The actor and Trump appeared engrossed in deep conversation, after which they shook hands, and Trump gave the actor an affectionate pat on the hand!

- Social media went into an uproar. People denigrated the actor, vowing never to watch any of his movies *ever* again. The hashtag *#complicit* took off. One fan even tweeted: "Shaking the hand of the man who colluded w/foreign leaders against his own country, instituted a law that lead to kidnapping & deaths of young children, recklessly brought America near to war & resulted in the deaths of 176 ppl shot down in retaliation."

- Trump supporters struck back, accusing people on "the left" of being intolerant of those who have different political viewpoints. Shortly after the clip went viral, the man who shot and posted the video began receiving death threats.

- After the usual hubbub and one-upmanship settled, a question arose for social media "experts" to ponder: *What in the heck were the two talking about, anyway?*

- It's no secret that this man is one of the rare, demonstrably right-wing actors in the predominantly liberal Hollywood community. But maybe he's just an over-zealous Republican, and his meeting with Trump meant nothing else at all. Perhaps he's just honored to meet a president. *Any* president.

- Lacking any actual proof of this actor's swamp status, we've yet to refer to him as one of Trump's swamp creatures. However, there are *indications* that this guy might not mind getting down and dirty in Trump's swamp. He certainly seems to *fit in.*

- In 2001 the actor got himself mixed up in a bar brawl and was arrested for assault. They eventually dropped those charges against him, but years later the cops nabbed this guy on suspicion of driving under the influence. He and an unidentified male passenger were uncooperative with the police and, at first, refused even to exit the vehicle.

- This actor's public views on gun control coincide with what the NRA commanded their puppet Trump to say. The actor spoke out against gun-free school zones, claiming that shootings only occur in schools that "don't allow guns." The actor even commented: *"Banning guns is like banning forks in an attempt to stop making people fat."*

- *HUH?*

- Since the powers that be in Hollywood weren't exactly tripping over each other with job offers for this actor, the man reinvented himself. And much of his latest work seems right up Trump's alley.

- The actor collaborated with Glenn Beck (right-wing political commentator, conspiracy theorist, and the guy who once wanted to blow his brains out to the tune of Kurt Cobain) to produce a "documentary" series.

- This possible wannabe swamp dweller also was the executive producer for a Netflix animated series that showcased a loudmouth white guy not happy about the rise of political correctness.

- The actor has starred in violent exploitation films by Craig Zahler, filmmaker and heavy metal artist. These movies have been labeled *unwoke racist fantasias*. Critics J. Hoberman and Manohla Dargis from *The New York Times* have expressed that these films espouse a mix of Breitbartian "white male grievance" represented by the casual bigotry of the characters, and "old-fashioned American anti-authoritarianism – with its hatred for rules matched only by a love of guns."

- *Trump's kind of movies*. Films that are also enjoyed by many of Trump's followers.

- This actor has also been working with and hanging around with Mel Gibson – the talented, once well-respected actor/director who sabotaged his own career when *he* got arrested for DUI. During the arrest, Gibson asked one of the officers if he was a Jew, proclaiming that: "The Jews are responsible for all the wars in the world!" He also couldn't resist calling the female arresting officer, "Sugar tits!"

- Trump's wheels had to be spinning during his conversation with the actor at that college football game. Imagine such a raw talent as this actor, combined with the brilliance of a man like Mel Gibson, channeled into making a movie to honor Trump. A film that would espouse all of Trump's "ideals" and portray Trump as the perpetual innocent victim. But Trump would look *oh so powerful too* . . . the man who would never quit – would never let us down – the tough as nails, very stable genius who would *forever* be our king!

- While most of Hollywood's denizens loathe Trump, this actor and Mel Gibson appear to resonate closely with Trump's vibrations. After Meryl Streep took Trump to task for mocking a disabled reporter during the Golden Globes awards, the audience wildly applauded. Gibson and this actor silently glared toward the stage.

- Think it's too far-fetched that Trump might dream of collaborating with this actor and Gibson on a movie that sings his praises? Think again. Trump's own former chief strategist, Steve Bannon, once dreamed about Gibson making *his* movie. Allegedly, Bannon even met with Gibson. Parts of the imagined film included segments about race and class subjugation – especially against Jews and Gypsies.

- Bannon is likely still lamenting that his eleven-page movie outline never made it past the trash heap. But Trump has a way of *making* things happen. Maybe we *do* know what Trump discussed with our mystery actor.

- *Coming soon to a theatre, or some sort of streaming device, near you?*

<u>**SWAMP DWELLER NUMBER NINE**</u>

- While we're on the subject of drunk drivers, let's turn our attention to another Trump reptile that the cops nabbed for that crime. They pulled this woman over for speeding, and her blood test proved she'd been ingesting more than just the Xanax (earlier in the day) and the Zoloft (the night before) that she claimed.

- She'd not only been speeding while drunk, but she did her super-fast drunken driving under a suspended license.

- Somehow, she finagled a deal and got the charges against her reduced to a mere *reckless* driving, with probation. After being given such a phenomenal break, this reptile didn't even bother to pay her fines or complete her Mothers Against Drunk Driving program.

- The powers that be had to keep hauling this dweller's ass back into court.

- Not one to show remorse, two years later authorities nabbed her again for driving without working headlights and suspicion of driving drunk. She didn't even bother to show up for her court hearing that time. Made the judge put out a warrant for her arrest.

- Once they finally landed this slippery reptile in court, she pleaded guilty. The court ordered her to check into a treatment program and pay fines and court costs.

- This snake once worked as a spokesperson for AAA, but it didn't take them long to fire her ass. Allegedly they caught her cheating on her expense reports.

- She had just about as much success in her next job at an advertising agency, where she got caught in a different type of cheating. At a meeting with the Office of Highway Safety, one of her clients showed off the "original" material on his website that this dweller had "created" for him. An attendee from AAA furiously informed the man that some of those materials had been plagiarized *verbatim* from *his* company's website. This swamp vermin got fired from that job as well.

- Somehow, after all that, she landed a job as a spokeswoman for her state's attorney general. Strange . . . most people with *her* background would have trouble even landing a job flipping burgers at a fast-food joint.

- Maybe similar personalities really do resonate. The man who gave this snake her break was under investigation himself for alleged campaign finance violations. When local reporters asked for public records related to her boss's case, this reptile told reporters their requests were "overreaching, an invasion of privacy and abusive use of your role in the media."

- While working in the state's attorney general's office, this dweller witnessed a botched state execution. After receiving a lethal injection, the convicted murderer snorted and gasped for air for just short of two hours before he finally expired. Witnesses counted at least several hundred of the man's wheezes. The execution went on for so long, the man's attorneys filed emergency appeals to save him. The incident was so brutal, a renowned appellate judge called for the return of the firing squad. But Trump's future snake described the execution as "quite peaceful" adding, "There was no gasping of air. There was snoring. He just laid there."

- According to *The Capitol Times,* (that was threatened with a lawsuit if they printed the story), our dweller took an unpaid leave from her job as spokeswoman for the Arizona House of Representatives to work on Trump's campaign. After Trump won the election, she should have returned to her position. Instead, she continued to work for Trump while collecting a full salary, $19,000 in taxpayer's money for eight weeks.

- While raking in her unearned money, she jetted around with Trump, enjoying her new position on his transition team. She flaunted countless pictures on her social media pages: her at Trump Tower; her many excursions to New York, Florida, New Jersey, Michigan, Maryland, Alabama, and Indiana; her at the Army/Navy football game with Trump; at Mar-a-Lago, where she couldn't resist bragging to her Facebook friends that for the next few days her office would be amongst the Florida palms! She even posted a photo of her luggage and shopping bags at a New York

City hotel and informed her followers: "This is what it looks like when you've lived in a hotel room for a few months."

- This dweller *did* return to her home state over that Thanksgiving holiday. But she couldn't have checked in at work – her office was closed.

- No one would imagine Trump would be stupid enough to give someone of this ilk a White House position. *Of course not!* He gave this dweller *three jobs*!

- This reptile started as the communications director for Melania Trump, where she immediately made use of her old cheating ways. She helped Melania launch "Be Best," the anti-opioid, anti-cyberbullying campaign. The program's signature pamphlet was nearly identical to a document that the Federal Trade Commission had released in 2014 under the Obama administration. The link on the White House webpage urged parents to read the booklet "Talking with Kids About Being Online," suggesting that *Melania* had written it – with a little help from the Federal Trade Commission.

- Eventually, the powers-that-be cleaned up the website to indicate that Melania had been merely *promoting* the information. When asked to comment about this *alleged* piracy, our reptile snapped: "I encourage members of the media to attempt to *Be Best* in their own professions."

- After the White House Press Secretary left her job (to head on over to Fox News, no surprise), Trump awarded this dweller with the press secretary's role in *addition* to the position of White House communications director. She also kept her original job with Melania. The Annual Report to Congress on White House Office Personnel formally listed this dweller as "assistant to the president and deputy chief of staff for communications for the first lady."

- Unfortunately, despite receiving an annual salary of at *least* $183,000, though this dweller plagiarized stuff and put out a litany of confrontational tweets and false statements, she never performed the duties of the job(s) the taxpayers paid her to do.

- One thing this snake *did* do was tweet a Trump campaign slogan – in direct violation of the Hatch Act.

- Traditionally the White House press secretary holds daily news conferences to keep America and the world informed; this dweller never held *one*. Her complete lack of doing her job caused a public Twitter altercation between her and authors Don Winslow and Stephen King. Collectively the authors offered to donate $200,000 to a children's charity if she would *only* hold a one-hour press briefing. In other words, they challenged her to *do her job* – at least once. The dweller lashed out at the authors, claiming that they should donate to children anyway, without strings attached. Both authors do regularly donate to charities. Unfortunately, their challenge to this dweller went nowhere.

- This dweller prefers to make her presence known through statements, print interviews, tweets, and on Fox News and other "safe" networks – where the hosts are usually Trump supporters.

- This dweller once bragged on Fox News: "We've got the best water and the best air in the world." She added that Trump is proud of that, and the two talk of this "achievement" often. That statement couldn't have been more false. In reality, since Trump continually makes it easier for his rich buddies to dump more and more poisons into our air and water every day, the quality of the essentials we need for our existence has become more toxic during Trump's reign. And yet – the Fox host never questioned the dweller on her bogus "facts." Instead, he immediately pivoted to crow about Melania's "spectacular" state dinner!

- This dweller misrepresented the truth when she informed the public (three *years* after Trump's inauguration) that the Obama administration had left behind (in the White House) a series of negative notes and messages for Trump and his crew. "I'll tell you something, *every* office was filled with Obama books, and we had notes left behind that said: 'You will fail,' 'You aren't going to make it,'" she insisted.

- Former members of the Obama administration vehemently denied this, detailing how they had left behind copious explanatory notes and countless words of encouragement. Trump's dweller backpedaled on her accusation after the Obama administration members provided copies of their positive letters. This snake provided zero proof of her allegations. She then claimed that she *certainly* wasn't implying that *every* office had that issue, adding that she couldn't understand why everyone was "so sensitive!"

- This critter lied when she claimed that during the impeachment hearings, the House was taking "secret, shady, closed-door depositions" from witnesses.

- After Vietnam veteran, U.S. Military Academy graduate and career diplomat William Taylor testified under oath during the impeachment proceedings, this dweller attacked him and the inquiry itself. She stated that it was a "coordinated smear campaign from far-left lawmakers and radical unelected bureaucrats waging war on the Constitution."

- Along with another swamp dweller, this snake published an opinion piece attacking *The Washington Post*, claiming the newspaper didn't cover specific stories about Trump's accomplishments. But The Post *did* cover the news they mentioned. The two swamp creatures even stated in their piece that there was "not a chance" that *The Washington Post* had written about the first time in history a sitting president walked across the DMZ into North Korea. Then they included a link – to that exact article – as it had appeared several months prior in *The Washington Post*. They had connected readers to the exact item that they had argued had "not a chance" of existing.

- The bog dweller attempted to justify backing up the pretend king at all costs by proclaiming: "It is literally my job to support and defend the president." *No*! *It is not!* Trump may wear the bootheels she had to lick to secure her power positions, but Trump never paid her salary. The American people did. And she had a responsibility to keep us informed of what was factually going on inside the White House. Not to throw a tarp over the swamp, to damn up the gurgling geysers of mud, to try to hide just how vile it is down there! Not to defend every vicious word that comes out of her boss's revolting mouth. Trump used OUR employee as HIS personal public relations person.

- This dweller knew precisely how to worm her way into Trump's swamp. She fought like a tiger to protect Trump, but when she sensed the obese old boy needed stroking, she kneeled before his pretend throne and made like an enamored, terrified kitten.

- After John Kelly, four-star Marine General and Trump's former chief of staff, claimed that he had warned Trump not to hire "yes men," this dweller retorted: "I worked with John Kelly, and he was totally unequipped to handle the genius of our great president."

- When Trump suggested deceased former Congressman John Dingell was in hell, this snake defended Trump, proclaiming that he was a counterpuncher who *had* to react – because he was "under attack." She neglected to explain how a guy who had been out of office for five years and dead for ten months had been attacking her boss.

- When Trump referred to "Never Trump" Republicans as human scum, this dweller expanded on the characterization: "The people who are against him, and who have been against him, and have been working against him since the day they took office are just that." She added that these people "deserve strong language like that."

- This creature from Trump's black lagoon not only demeans herself by lashing out with blatant lies meant solely to benefit Trump, but she also subjugates herself for the pretend king's personal pleasure. During a news conference with Trump and the South Korean president, one of the Korean hosts asked this dweller to select an American reporter to ask the next question. The dweller insisted: "I'm going to let our president choose." To which a smiling, smug Trump boasted: "She's learned very well."

<u>SWAMP DWELLER NUMBER TEN</u>

- This swamp dweller has had many public battles, starting decades ago, with alcohol and cocaine. His former employers forced him to resign from a top position in a financial organization because of his frequent drug and alcohol binges.

- Even recently, his slurs were so evident during a CNN interview, countless observers concluded he was having . . . *issues*.

- During this dweller's appearance on Fox News, the Twitterverse erupted. One Twitter user (a bartender for 30 years) offered her qualified opinion: "I gotta say this guy appears drunk."

- Social media users everywhere agreed this reptile was sloshed. Immediately this dweller rose in the ranks to become Trump's latest laughingstock.

- Amazingly Trump (who is supposedly appalled by those who overindulge and is incredibly intolerant of anyone who embarrasses him in public) allowed this tipsy varmint to keep on slithering through the swamp.

- We would have to assume that since a robust economy means the world to Trump, this dweller (the head of our National *Economic* Council) has to be doing a bang-up job!

- Perhaps that supposed bang-up job is beneficial to Trump? *Personally*?

- When Trump pushed his tax cut (that would mostly benefit the wealthy and prove especially favorable to Trump's personal businesses), the Congressional Budget Office (CBO) concluded that the tax cuts would increase our deficit by $1.3 *trillion*.

- Since the consensus among top professionals is that CBO's forecasts have been historically proven credible and without partisan intent, this dweller should have attempted to put the brakes on this tax cut. At least he should have considered how, in due course, his decision would likely inflict crisis upon the American people.

- Instead, the dweller proclaimed: "Never believe the CBO. Very important: Never believe them. They're always wrong, especially with regard to tax cuts, which they never score properly."

- The lizard also ignored the fact that every other credible study of Trump's upcoming tax plan also demonstrated how the program would drastically increase our deficit.

- The dweller continued to spread falsities about the tax cuts. He claimed that CBO's latest figures showed "the entire $1.5 trillion tax cut is virtually paid for by higher revenues and better nominal GDP." Experts, spokespersons for other agencies, and mainstream economists emphatically declared the opposite. In fact, the CBO later concluded that their original calculations of how much damage Trump's tax cuts would inflict upon our deficit were actually on the low side.

- This bottom-feeder has spread disproven theories (that ended up shifting even greater wealth to the wealthy) since his days as a TV commentator. No doubt, this is why Trump wanted him in his sinkhole in the first place and has no qualms about keeping him there – even though this dweller's financial predictions are almost always less than stellar.

- This dweller was wrong about the housing bubble and its aftermath.

- He predicted that President Clinton's tax increases would: "throw a blanket over the recovery and depress the economy's long-run potential to grow." The muddied creature made *that* brilliant declaration towards the beginning of the longest bull market in history. He then credited the strong market back to the Bush administration, even though it occurred long after Bush had left office.

- In March 2007, this reptile declared: "Former Federal Reserve Chairman, Alan Greenspan this week even predicted a recession, naming the budget deficit as the cause. *Huh*? The deficit is evaporating as record tax revenues are being generated by a solid economy, itself a function of the low marginal tax rates put in place by President Bush."

- He spouted this crap (the exact same BS he's feeding us now) just months before the Great Recession hit.

- Here's what he had to say when that downturn (the one he swore wasn't coming) actually did arrive: "Recessions are therapeutic. They cleanse excess from the economy. Think about excessive risk speculation, leverage, and housing. Recessions are curative. They restore balance and create the foundation for the next recovery."

- Did this reptile really believe that working-class families considered their ability to get credit, to keep their jobs, and stay in their homes were *excesses?* In need of . . . *cleansing?* Did they really look at losing their life savings as *therapeutic and curative?* Was their balance actually. . . *restored?*

- And yet, this lizard still spouts off his same rubbish. He tries to make us believe that Trump's tax cut has paid for itself, not admitting that Americans will pay for all those extra chunks of change rattling around in his and Trump's pockets for generations and generations to come.

- During the 2018 - 2019 partial federal shutdown, the government mandated that approximately 420,000 essential workers report to their jobs. They worked without pay. After 34 grueling days (without even the opportunity for these unpaid employees to seek income elsewhere), this dweller declared that these people were "volunteering" to work because they loved their country and because of their "allegiance" to Trump.

- After Trump ranted that Google was rigging its search results with information that was against him, the pretend king's loyal subject announced that they were "taking a look at" regulating the search engine.

- This lizard continues to defend Trump as he pushes to repeal an anti-corruption law, which would make it legal for U.S. businesses to bribe foreigners. But we need not worry about this since the dweller assured us: "wealthy folks have no need to steal or engage in corruption."

- Trump must really love this guy's current day loyalty and showbiz style of misleading the public. Apparently, Trump forgave what this dweller said back in 2015: "And let's not forget: the stock market, which is a leading indicator of the future economy, is in a wee bit of a correction. Given the recent rise of presidential candidate Donald Trump, we should all be thankful that stocks haven't plunged. Trump's agenda of trade protectionism, dollar devaluation, and immigrant deportation is completely anti-growth. It's like Fortress America in an economy that is completely globalized and where the U.S. must compete in the worldwide race for capital and labor. Trump's policies don't fit."

CHAPTER THREE ~

A FEW MORE DRUNKS

Although Trump claims to have an aversion to drunkards, he's flooded his swamp with dipsomaniacs. In fact, because of the loose lips of Trump's foreign policy adviser, while on a bender in an upscale London bar, that establishment became the birthplace of the Mueller investigation. See if you can spot that dweller in this continuation list of some of Trump's boozehounds – or maybe he's *not* included here. It's good to keep you guessing!

SWAMP DWELLER NUMBER ELEVEN

- This snake, the Swamp King's first campaign manager, enjoys frequent access to the Trump White House and has built a roster of significant lobbyists as his clients.

- Countless people have described this dweller as brash, ambitious, relentless, ruthless, aggressive, a bomb-thrower, shady, a cowboy, a hothead, a bully, a condescending and nasty brutish boor, quick-tempered and heavy-handed. Even with all his off-putting qualities, this dweller demands loyalty.

- Subsisting on little sleep, he derives his energy from constantly chug-a-lugging Red Bull and Monster energy drinks.

- Long before this reptile nosedived into Trump's swamp, he had been out in the world, stirring up trouble.

- One of his first jobs was working for a congressman who'd been sentenced on federal corruption charges. In a letter to a judge, this dweller asked for leniency for the congressman, claiming he considered him a mentor and "surrogate father."

- In 1999 this dweller hauled a laundry bag, with a loaded handgun inside, into the Longworth House Office Building.

- When arrested, he had three pistol magazines and several rounds of ammunition on him.

- Even after this snake was lucky enough to have the charges against him eventually dropped, he still fought – for four years – to get his gun and ammo back.

- The dweller also pushed to have his court fees reimbursed.

- He even insisted that the courts throw in an additional fifty grand for his pain and suffering. He obviously felt it was the duty of U.S. taxpayers to compensate him for the *anguish* he must have endured after being deprived of the company of his gun!

- His co-workers at Americans for Prosperity (AFP), (an advocacy group backed by the Koch Brothers), where the dweller also worked, weren't overly fond of this dweller.

- This reptile allegedly threatened to blow up the chief financial officer's car because his expense reimbursement check was late.

- When one man missed a conference call with the dweller to be with his dying grandmother, this snake called to chew the man out. While the man's grandmother was having last rites administered, the dweller demanded to know who the hell the man thought he was for missing the conference call.

- Another of the reptile's prior coworkers stated that this dweller threatened to *come down really hard* on her if she didn't muster up at least 50 people to attend an event.

- Another woman claimed that this bottom-feeder: ". . . gets on the phone and defames my character. He called me incompetent, called me a loser. He called me a f**king b**ch, yelling, 'I am going to fire your f**king ass!'"

- During this dweller's time with AFP, reports emerged about him being rough with journalists, sexually suggestive with female reporters, and profanely berating of anyone he thought might try to test his authority.

- In front of a group of employees, including senior officials, this dweller scolded a female employee calling her a "c**t."

- After that incident, the powers that be shifted this muddied life form into another role where he oversaw a multi-state voter registration drive. Under this dweller's direction, the organization sent incorrect voter registration forms to residents.

- Also, while this dweller was running registration efforts, authorities investigated the group for voter suppression. Some mailers sent out under this dweller's charge provided incorrect voter registration deadlines, the wrong address to send registration forms to, and inaccurate contact information for follow-up inquiries. Other mailers wrongly instructed registered voters that they could lose eligibility in the upcoming election if they didn't re-register. More than once, they sent mailers to children and dead people. They even solicited a house cat.

- Shortly after his fiasco job with AFP, this snake hooked up with Donald Trump's election campaign and started up with more of the same.

- He allegedly grabbed a female reporter who had tried to ask Trump a question.

- Reporters gave this reptile the moniker "Trump's top goon."

- Trump's own staff and advisers planned a coup against this dweller during the campaign but called it off after Trump started to do well in the polls.

- Another woman filed a police complaint against the dweller, claiming he slapped her rear end at a holiday party held at Trump's Washington, D.C. hotel. Allegedly after she threatened to report the dweller for sexual harassment, the snake responded, "I work in the private sector," just before slapping her again.

- Other reports surfaced of this amphibious critter physically pushing reporters away from candidate Trump.

- Journalists claimed that this dweller had consistently made vulgar and sexually suggestive comments to and about female reporters.

- Despite a video showing this dweller grabbing a protestor by the collar during one of Trump's campaign events, the dweller denied having done so.

- During a televised event, the snake insisted that the Mueller report showed *no collusion, no obstruction.* The host pointed out that the

Mueller report did not say that. To which the dweller insisted, "it absolutely says that," just before admitting he'd never read the report and accusing the reporter (who *had* read the entire account) of not reading it either.

- The muddied creature even claimed the reporter was lying and being disingenuous when she correctly pointed out that the Mueller report contained at least ten different examples of Trump's obstruction of justice.

- At one point the dweller asked, "Are you a journalist, or are you a talking head?"

- The Mueller report included information about how Trump involved this dweller in his attempt to fire Attorney General Jeff Sessions for recusing himself from the Russia/Trump campaign investigation. Trump had even asked this dweller to fire Sessions himself. Much of the background information in the Mueller report had come from this amphibious creature's own testimony.

- The dweller later stated he couldn't remember any of the incidents, even though he had testified about them under oath during the Mueller investigation. "I don't ever remember the president ever asking me to get involved with Jeff Sessions or the Department of Justice in any way, shape, or form ever," he insisted.

- When questioned by the House Judiciary Committee about the discrepancies between what he testified to in the Mueller investigation and his comments to the media, the dweller replied: "I have no obligation to be honest with the media because they're just as dishonest as anyone else."

- The snake cheated on his wife, having an extramarital affair with Hope Hicks, the former White House communications director and current adviser to Trump.

- During a Fox News appearance, when a guest mentioned a young child with Down syndrome who, (under the Trump administration's family separation policy), had been forced from her mother's arms and allegedly thrown into a cage, this dweller replied, "womp, womp."

- In a subsequent television appearance, the dweller blew off an opportunity to apologize, claiming (contrary to governmental evidence) that the separated child's mother was likely a member of a child-smuggling ring.

- This reptile withdrew from his Senate campaign in New Hampshire but couldn't resist tweeting: "I am certain I would have won."

- This dweller appeared so out of his skull one night during a Fox News interview that even the host, from the network that is usually friendly to Trump's goons, couldn't help asking, "did you have a little Merlot with dinner?" The host eventually cut the dweller off, suggesting he get a cup of coffee.

SWAMP DWELLER NUMBER TWELVE

- This dweller lied on his LinkedIn page about the dates he attended college.

- After *The Washington Post* raised some questions about the accuracy of this alligator's online posts, he removed the dates about his education. He took down another claim that he'd been a Marine recruiter.

- The dweller claimed the posts were merely mistakes and then, in true Trumpian fashion, threw his relative under the bus, claiming that relative had created the LinkedIn page for him.

- This alligator once punched a man in the back of the head then ran away from the police. When officers eventually caught up with him, they charged him with disorderly conduct, assault, and resisting arrest.

- In a separate incident, the police charged this dweller with underage drinking.

- The powers that be dismissed that charge under a first offender's program. But not long after, the police charged this alligator with disorderly conduct. The dweller had gotten into a fight around 2 a.m., shortly after leaving a hookah bar. He punched his fist through a glass door, then wandered off, leaving a trail of blood in his wake.

- Nepotism should not play a part in any well-drained swamp, yet Trump didn't seem to mind that this guy's cousin brought him into the fold. Despite this dweller's dishonest ways and volatile past, or maybe *because of* all that, Trump hired him for his campaign.

- After Trump won the election, and the swamp put this guy through their usual *vetting* (or lack thereof), they gave him a position in the White House personnel office. Trump allowed this dweller with the checkered past to be in charge of selecting and placing appointees to agencies such as Veterans Affairs, the Department of Homeland Security, and the Defense Department.

- In 2019 the Swamp administration promoted this muddied creature to special deputy assistant to Trump and director of the Office of Presidential Advance with a salary of at least $158,000.

SWAMP DWELLER NUMBER THIRTEEN

- People who've worked with this dweller don't seem to like him very much. Here's what some of his former co-workers said about him: The day-to-day environment was like "walking on eggshells," with a "constant fear of reprisal." This snake was "the most unethical person I have ever worked with," he was "the worse leader I've ever worked for," he was "incapable of not losing his temper." Working in the same agency as this dweller was the "worst experience of my life," to another it was her "worst assignment," another described this dweller as "the worst officer I have ever served with," and still others proclaimed he was someone who "would roll over anyone." He "worked his way up on the backs of others," he had "screaming tantrums," and "screaming fits," he was a "suck up to those above him and abusive to those below him." He was a "kiss up, kick down boss," he had "100 percent bad temper," "screaming tantrums," and "screaming fits." He "put his needs above everyone else's," and he would "lose his mind over small things."

- This bottom-feeder's peers have also described him as flat-out unethical, intolerable, belittling, vindictive, explosive, toxic, abusive, despicable, dishonest, and volatile.

- Trump described this dweller as "one of the finest people that I have met."

- This snake was once the White House physician, and Trump undoubtedly was happy with how this doctor provided him with sterling public reports after his physical exams. The doctor also graded Trump a perfect score on a test designed to detect any cognitive impairments.

- Despite a complete lack of qualifications for the position, or perhaps *because of* this and the man's abrasive personality, Trump nominated this dweller to be the secretary of veterans affairs.

- Shortly after the nomination, allegations against the snake surfaced.

- In separate interviews, many individuals explained that this reptile's peers had nicknamed him "Candyman" since he allegedly handed out prescription medicine like it was candy, bypassing all required intakes, questionnaires, and paperwork.

- The dweller would frequently provide paperwork *after the fact* to account for shortages of controlled substances.

- A co-worker revealed this swamp vermin wrote scripts for himself. After he got caught doing so, he delegated that task to his *personal assistant.*

- He wrote prescriptions for sleep aids for people who weren't even taking those medications, to protect those who were.

- Prior co-workers described multiple incidents where this dweller was drunk while on duty.

- This snake was often on call in case of any health issues with the president. Observers had stated that he frequently appeared inebriated during these times, and at least once, co-workers found him passed out drunk when he was needed.

- Some claimed that during a party for the Secret Service members, this dweller got so drunk he wrecked a government vehicle.

- CNN reported that one time, while this amphibious critter was ultra inebriated, he made so much noise knocking on a woman's hotel room door that Secret Service agents had to step in to prevent him from possibly waking up then-President Barack Obama. Under the Trump administration, the Secret Service later stated they did not have any specific record of this incident.

- After these and countless other allegations surfaced, the nomination for secretary of veteran's affairs was withdrawn. But that didn't stop Trump from lashing out at the dweller's "critics." He even demanded the resignation of a senator who merely did his job of screening nominees by bringing several of the charges against this dweller to light.

- Though it was common knowledge that many who knew this reptile found him to be unethical, intolerable, belittling, vindictive, explosive, toxic, abusive, despicable, dishonest, and volatile,

Trump promoted him to assistant to the president and chief White House medical adviser.

- Trump also requested that the Senate promote this snake from rear admiral to two-star admiral.

- Though under continuing investigation by the inspector general's office, this dweller left the White House and retired from the Navy. Typically, military officials under such investigations are prohibited from withdrawing until the completion of any probes against them.

- A spokesperson for the inspector general's office stated that conducting the investigation has been challenging. The White House has kept a watchful eye on all requests for information and interviews. Nothing can move forward in the inquiry without approval from Trump's swamp.

<u>**SWAMP DWELLER NUMBER FOURTEEN**</u>

- After a stint as a body man during Trump's campaign, Trump gave this dweller a position (for which he was not qualified) in security and operations at the Department of Homeland Security.

- In the dweller's own words: "I was one of those knucklehead kids growing up who got straight C's and D's. I was on welfare. I never went to college, and I should have been one of those kids that ends up in jail or doing dishes somewhere."

- As with many other swamp dwellers, court documents show that this alligator had been charged with driving or attempting to drive while drunk.

- Soon after joining the Department of Homeland Security, this dweller settled a long outstanding tax lien of nearly eight grand.

- During his time in the swamp, this reptile never filed the required financial disclosure forms. This rare and severe offense, in prior cases, has resulted in criminal charges by the Justice Department.

- Despite this dweller's lack of cooperation, or maybe *because of* the dweller's rebellious tendencies, Trump chose to promote him to deputy chief of staff of operations at the Environmental Protection Agency (EPA). The dweller's actions should have precipitated dismissal, fines, and criminal charges. Instead, this unqualified, non-college graduate received a senior executive salary of at least $140,000.

- *So, this alligator was unqualified, overpaid, and an apparent deadbeat who thought following the rules was beneath him. In other words, he was just another typical Trump swamp dweller. But then things got a bit . . . sticky.*

- This dweller appeared (at one point at least, and for reasons unproven) to actually be attempting to *drain* the swamp.

- After his attempts to rein in illicit spending in his department failed, this alligator helped expose Scott Pruitt (then head of the EPA) for his excessive travel and spending practices.

- Because Trump always insists – *all the murky dealings that happen in the swamp must stay hidden in the bog* – the Swamp administration soon asked this dweller to resign. Trump's team also demoted several other dwellers who had come forward about Pruitt's indiscretions.

- Swamp officials claimed they fired the alligator because he was often unresponsive while on trips.

- Someone filed an anonymous complaint against the dweller, stating that he could not get the appropriate security clearance because of his various indiscretions. Allegations against the alligator were investigated and dismissed.

- Once the alligator came forward with accusations of misconduct against Pruitt, mainstream and left-leaning news sources coveted interviews with the dweller and published mainly positive stories about him.

- Right-wing publications (which included several with questionable histories and dubious sources) showed no mercy to the dweller. Some of their reporting could well have been accurate (heck countless swamp creatures *have* proven themselves to be more than a little unsavory). But these sources could have easily manufactured or distorted much of what they had alleged. Trump's buddies in the press wouldn't think twice about demeaning this whistleblower solely to provide another layer of slime cover for Trump's swamp.

- Following is a bit of what those questionable right-wing sources had to say about the dweller. The "information" (*in italics*) is not readily available in mainstream publications. Either some (or all of) these innuendos might not be true. If they are, then perhaps multiple mainstream media sources prefer to keep the whistleblower looking more pristine than he might actually be.

- *The dweller refused to hand over his placard and government ID badge when requested to do so.*

- *As previously mentioned, sources reported that the dweller could not get the proper security clearance.*

- *The alligator claimed to have Top Secret security clearance but would not provide the proper paperwork to the press.*

- *Outfitted with police lights so he could speed through slow traffic, this reptile drove around in a phony police cruiser.*

- *The EPA pushed the dweller out for impersonating a police officer.*

- *Swamp bosses listed the dweller as officially AWOL in the government.*

- *After hiring an American Idol contestant to sing the National Anthem at Trump rallies, the dweller had an extramarital affair with her.*

- *This alligator did not inform his mistress he was married, then later lied to her, claiming he was getting a divorce.*

- *The dweller paraded this woman around on his arm in front of Trump's entire campaign staff even though they all knew he had a wife at home.*

- *After the mistress ditched the dweller, when she learned about his marital status, he refused to book her again to sing at any pro-Trump events.*

- *She claimed he lied about being a Navy Seal.*

- *The reptile called up this former mistress and threatened her, insisting she must not speak with the press.*

- *He intentionally plotted to have Pruitt and Zinke removed from their jobs.*

- *The alligator also threatened a reporter, vowing he'd target the reporter for the remainder of his career.*

- *Fellow campaign workers stated they became alarmed after witnessing the dweller shoving protesters at Trump rallies.*

- *Sources stated that, after Trump's swamp administration fired this dweller, he threatened to go public with his allegations against Pruitt. Another source published e-mails allegedly proving that the swamp bosses "nudged" the alligator to retire immediately **after** the story broke.*

- *A former co-worker and childhood friend allegedly stated that this dweller is a pathological liar and lied about his service length in the Coast Guard when seeking a job with the Trump campaign. The dweller also, according to his "friend," went AWOL from the Coast Guard.*

- *Newsmax* is one of the organizations that came down incredibly hard on this alligator after he exposed some of the wrongdoing inside Trump's swamp.

- The founder, CEO, and president of *Newsmax* is a close friend to Trump.

SWAMP DWELLER NUMBER FIFTEEN

- Trump had nominated this "winner" (with zero governmental experience) to be our labor secretary. The nomination never went through.

- This man has proven in so many ways to be a true enemy of the working class. In spite of, or maybe *because of* this disconnect, Trump wanted this dweller in a position typically reserved for advocates of the working people.

- This snake once worked at a law firm owned by a famous mob lawyer whom the Department of Labor accused of skimming $25 million from his worker's pension funds to use on bogus investments.

- This reptile defended his boss during the trial by attacking the government, claiming that the overzealous Washington regulators were to blame for his boss not paying back the money to his employees.

- Later, as the chief executive of CKE Restaurants, (Carl's Jr., and Hardee's parent company), this dweller argued that labor regulations were to blame for stifling economic growth.

- He referred to his own employees as "the best of the worst."

- Those workers filed frequent labor lawsuits against CKE Restaurants.

- His employees have also claimed on-the-job harassment.

- This reptile is not only dead set against raising the minimum wage, but there were also numerous wage violations throughout his restaurants. Often, he didn't even pay his employees minimum wage.

- His company blocked investigators from speaking to those workers.

- He has criticized paid sick leave policies.

- This dweller, Trump's choice to help uplift the working-class, also wanted to automate fast-food businesses. He argued that machines are "always polite, they always upsell, they never take a vacation, they never show up late, there's never a slip-and-fall or an age, sex or race discrimination case."

- This snake also hired an undocumented, illegal immigrant to do his housework, thus bypassing all labor and wage laws and avoiding forking over payroll taxes.

- CKE Restaurants has frequently run ads featuring scantily clad women to which the dweller commented: "I like beautiful women eating burgers in bikinis. I think it's very American."

- The bottom-feeder also liked beating up beautiful women. His ex-wife claimed she called the police because "he assaulted and battered me by striking me violently about the face, chest, back, shoulders and neck, without provocation or cause," leaving "bruises and contusions to the chest, back, shoulders and neck" and, among other injuries, "two ruptured discs and two bulging discs." She later retracted her statement as part of a child custody agreement.

- His ex-wife also claimed that after she made her allegations public, the dweller vowed: "I will see you in the gutter. This will never be over. You will pay for this."

- The snake was accused of pummeling his wife in the car after being spotted driving erratically.

- Though this tidbit was not found in many mainstream publications, after denying that he beat his wife, his alleged defense for driving recklessly was that he had merely been *driving drunk*!

- This reptile wrote a book, grumbling that he didn't get approved for his position in the swamp because of a progressive smear campaign against him, which was an act of desperation from the left-wing that is facing irrelevance because Trump, who is pro-business, is in the White House.

CHAPTER FOUR ~

COMMUNICATIONS REPTILES

The president of the United States typically surrounds himself with communications *experts*. Ideally, these men and women are highly educated and well-trained in the field. They come into their positions with tons of experience and possess a top-level of integrity. They also know how to speak respectfully to reporters and are empathetic towards the American people. We expect members of the White House communications team to gather *facts* of what is happening in the administration, the country, and the world, and relay those *facts* entirely and honestly to reporters and thus to the American people. Sometimes, for the sake of national security, they might have to be a bit elusive or even tell a few tiny white lies. But overall, the president looks for people for the communications team that will be purveyors of the truth. This is as it *should* be.

Historically some White House communications personnel have been better at their jobs than others. Certain individuals may not have been as personable as Americans might have liked. Maybe they didn't get along all that well with the press. The press core's primary functions are getting the truth, getting the scoop, and getting people to consume their product. Sometimes they might not seem like the nicest people in the world either.

But overall, the process has been the same. Reporters ask questions. Reporters get honest answers, or at least answers that are as forthcoming as possible.

That's the way it's always been . . . *until now*.

The majority of historians agree – Trump is running the most dishonest White House in American history. Never have Americans seen the extreme level of brutality, animosity, and dishonesty that this White House dishes out to reporters and the American people on a regular basis.

When Trump hires people for his communications team, he doesn't give one whit about their education level, experience, or scruples. Actually, in rethinking that, he probably *does* care about their scruples; he eagerly hires swamp creatures who don't have any.

Mostly Trump looks for people who are not afraid to check their integrity at the door. His ideal underlings never flinch when lying straight-faced for him. These people (when asked a question that Trump doesn't want answered because it will make him look bad) will boldly lash out at the person who *dared* to ask such a question. They always put the questioners on the defense and try to make it look as if *they* are guilty of something.

Trump obviously doesn't mind when his "communications" people don't even bother to face reporters or address the public. We've already "met" one of those dwellers in another category. *Remember the drunken communications reptile who considered it beneath her to attend those mandatory drunk driving courses?* In her tenure as Trump's frontline communications person, she never even once held a press conference.

That didn't matter, though. Very few of Trump's communications dwellers, even when they do hold press conferences, have ever legitimately answered any of the questions that the press members have asked.

Another fundamental technique of Trump's swamp communicators is the use of "keywords." Watch them in action. They have template answers in their notes that they read every time they hear specific keywords. Once a reporter mentions that word, a Trump communications person cuts that person off mid-question and reads the template answer connected to that word. They seldom let the inquirer finish his or her question. Often times, their boilerplate response has nothing to do with what the original question might have been. And when Trump's communications dwellers suspect a reporter wants to finish asking that damaging question or has a similar follow-up question, they'll immediately cut the reporter off again. Then whenever another reporter starts a question that has the same keyword in it, though that question might be entirely different from the one the prior reporter had attempted to ask, the dweller, after sighing impatiently and leading with "AGAIN," or "I'll REPEAT myself," or AS I'VE SAID MANY times," in a huffy manner to show how annoyed they are at hearing the "same" question, will read the boilerplate answer all over again. Thus they can make it appear, to some people at least, that it's all the reporter's fault for not paying attention to the "answer" the first time. The dwellers even manage to fool some members of the unsuspecting public into believing that the question *had* been answered and the "fake news, aggressive" reporters are harassing *them*.

Be sure to watch for these tactics from Trump's communications reptiles – if ever you can catch one of them talking to the press.

In this chapter, you'll learn about five of Trump's communications reptiles. See if you can guess their identities.

SWAMP DWELLER NUMBER SIXTEEN

- At least this dweller has a sense of humor. After lasting less than two weeks in the Trump administration, this swamp creature went on Stephen Colbert's show and proclaimed: "I thought I'd last longer than a carton of milk."

- Unlike many swamp creatures (who depart the central marshlands then almost immediately land lucrative positions in Trump's 2020 campaign, courtesy of Trump's donors), this man is no longer a swamp enthusiast. Nowadays, he campaigns voraciously *against* Trump.

- But for ages after his firing, this lizard staunchly defended Trump. He praised his ex-boss so prolifically on TV, it seemed as if he was auditioning for yet another gig in the swamp. (Countless swamp dwellers have landed their positions in the mud by singing Trump's praises on cable TV. They know their wannabe king is always watching and sucks in their praises almost as fast as he does his double cheeseburgers and milkshake chasers.)

- No matter how loud this particular dweller broadcast his clarion call, it became increasingly clear that Trump had permanently spit him out from the swamp.

- The genuine animosity between the two men began after this dweller sprinkled an unfavorable remark about Trump into his usual lavish praise during an episode of Real Time with Bill Maher. The bog dweller even exclaimed: "I do try to defend (Trump), but there are certain things he's done that are absolutely indefensible."

- Specifically, this dweller was critical of Trump's trips to El Paso, Texas, and Dayton, Ohio, where he met with survivors of mass shootings. This lizard described Trump's visit to an El Paso hospital as a "catastrophe," citing a video that showed Trump talking more about himself and his crowd sizes than comforting and honoring the survivors, first responders, and medical workers.

- Trump raced to Twitter to attack the man who had been one of his staunchest defenders. He tweeted that his swamp had terminated this dweller from a position that the lizard was incapable of handling and that it now seems as if the dweller does nothing but go on television as the all-time expert on Trump! He added, "Like many other so-called television experts, he knows very little about me." Trump then touted that his administration has done more than any other administration. He claimed that this reptile would do anything to get back into the swamp and implied that he (Trump) was the only reason this dweller could even get on television in the first place.

That left three questions begging for answers:

1. No matter how many times this reptile exhaustively defended Trump in the past, Trump couldn't forgive him even one honest, constructive criticism?

2. If the dweller was incapable of handling his position, why did Trump (who hires only the best) allow him into the coveted swamp in the first place?

3. *Trump watches Bill Maher?*

- The lizard quickly responded: "For the last three years, I have fully supported this president. Recently he has said things that divide the country in a way that is unacceptable. So, I didn't make the 100% litmus test. Eventually, he turns on everyone, and soon it will be you and then the entire country." The former swamp inhabitant made several more disparaging remarks about Trump, even proclaiming that Trump was "akin to a melting nuclear reactor."

- Before their Twitter war, this dweller was saying: "I love the guy." After Trump attacked him on Twitter, he started referring to Trump as a crazy, narcissistic "jackass."

- A swift change of heart on the dweller's part after a couple of typical, pathetically predictable Trump tweets! The lizard should have expected as much, especially since he appeared to claim to know Trump inside out.

- This soggy creature seemed always to be a walking lesson in contradictions.

- Before hooking up with Trump, this dweller declared: "The science of climate change is pretty much irrefutable at this point, and I find it tragic that so many people in this country believe global warming is some sort of elaborate hoax perpetuated by every credible scientist on the planet." In that statement, he likely was referring to Trump, who has asserted that climate change is a hoax invented by the Chinese.

- After diving into Trump's sinkhole, this dweller's climate change declarations took a sharp turn. "There are scientists that believe that that's not happening," he said. Even after being reminded that the scientific consensus is that humans are causing the climate to change, this dweller added: "there was overwhelming science that the earth was flat and there was an overwhelming science that we were the center of the world."

- Before this lizard dropped his anchor down into the swamp, he littered his Twitter account with tons of anti-Trump sentiment. At one point, he even tweeted out a picture of the Berlin Wall with his opinion: "Walls don't work. Never have never will. The Berlin Wall 1961-1989 don't fall for it."

- This former swamp inhabitant had supported Obama AND Hillary. He'd also endorsed Republicans Scott Walker and Jeb Bush while calling Trump a "hack politician" whose rhetoric is "anti-American and very, very divisive." He even added, for his television audience, "I'll tell you who he's going to be president of. You can tell Donald I said this: The Queens County Bullies Association. You're an inherited money dude from Queens County. Bring it, Donald. Bring it."

- Not too long after making those comments, and after Scott Walker and Jeb Bush were no longer in the running for president, the dweller joined Trump's Finance Committee.

- After securing a higher position in the White House, the lizard held an introductory news conference. He had this to say about Trump: "I was in the Oval Office with him earlier today, and we were talking about letting him be himself, letting him express his full identity. I think he's got some of the best political instincts in the world and perhaps in history."

- The dweller then raced to delete his plethora of negative Trump tweets. He claimed he had to do it, "in the name of transparency."

- Strange how it never occurred to such an intelligent man (Trump hires only the best) who was running for a *communications* position inside the White House, to delete those telltale tweets a trifle sooner.

- Once on the job, this communications swamp guy really went to work for Trump. He promised he would find the sources of the White House leaks and rid the administration of disloyal aides! By his fourth day in the White House, he went as far as to announce:

"I'm going to fire everybody!" He even named one staffer directly, who quickly resigned after the announcement.

- The biggest upset of this bottom-feeder's brief swamp career was a recorded telephone conversation he had with Ryan Lizza, a reporter for *The New Yorker*. The dweller blamed Reince Priebus (The Swamp's chief of staff at the time) for all the negative publicity he had gotten while on the job. His word choices were so tasteless and offensive, we won't repeat them here. Think about that! What this dweller said was too filthy even for a book about some of the nastiest, murkiest, and swampiest swamp people that ever existed.

- The reptile also bellowed vicious expletives while altering his voice to mimic Priebus. He used vulgar sexual imagery in attacking Trump's chief strategist, Steve Bannon.

- At one point, the lizard even declared: "What I want to do is I want to f***ing *kill* all the leakers, and I want to get the president's agenda on track so we can succeed for the American people."

- Though this dweller purportedly never told the reporter their conversation was off the record, once the reporter released the call to the public, this dweller tweeted that he would never mistakenly trust a journalist again.

- But shortly after his declaration of complete mistrust of reporters, the dweller started appearing on countless television broadcasts, talking to *journalists* – the exact people he mistrusted so much.

- After this swampy creature falsely implied that Priebus had committed a felony, then White House spokeswoman Sarah Huckabee Sanders gave this dweller (her boss at the time) a thumbs-up! She said that Trump "likes that type of competition and encourages it."

For the record: Trump did admit that he watched Bill Maher that fateful night! But (and he felt it essential to clarify) he watched it purely "by accident."

SWAMP DWELLER NUMBER SEVENTEEN

- Here's a dweller who just can't get her "facts" straight. During the 2016 presidential campaign, she claimed that Hillary Clinton suffered from a rare medical condition known as dysphasia, a brain illness. Clinton does not. Never did. Not even close.

- This swamp creature, who has zero medical training, made this up and decided (even though the lie could harm Clinton's campaign) that she would broadcast her "diagnosis" on a major television network.

- The dweller also alleged that members of the media have "literally beat Trump supporters into submission." A total and complete fabrication.

- Another false claim of hers was that President Obama started the war in Afghanistan. It obviously didn't matter to her that Obama was a state senator in Illinois at the time. Was she outright and intentionally lying, ill-informed, or just plain didn't give a damn?

- When asked to clarify her false comments, she dug in: "That was Obama's war, yes," she insisted.

- At some point, she must have eventually realized that nearly everyone was on to her blatantly false accusations as she later tried to blame "audio disruptions" for her misrepresentations.

- Remember the Gold Star family at the Democratic Convention that Trump felt it necessary to antagonize? During another television interview, this dweller blamed their son's death during the Iraq war on President Obama and Hillary Clinton. Never mind that Bush was president at the time when the tragic death occurred. Neither Obama nor Clinton could have had any influence on the tragic death.

- And so on, this woman spread conspiracy theories and other fantastical imaginings. Hashtags and parody accounts sprung up on Twitter; users mercilessly mocked her.

- One cannot imagine any "normal" prominent man of the world wanting someone like her to represent him. Any such lying, uninformed person who'd become a laughingstock like this woman should definitely not be considered for a position. And yet – Trump chose this bottom-feeder to be his 2016 national campaign spokesperson. And guess what, folks? She's back for Trump's 2020 campaign as his senior adviser.

- Could it be her super-duper suitable education that got her hired? Not likely. Her degrees are in science and biology.

- Could it be her demonstrated loyalty? Also, not likely. This reptile voted for Obama. But then she began favoring the tea party because Obama didn't regularly wear an American flag on his lapel. So – what was it then? Why would Trump grant this confused, lying, ridiculed woman a position in his campaign? Representing him to the public no less?

- Trump has an affinity for people who don't think twice about boldly presenting untruths to the world – especially when those outright lies stand to benefit him. Plus, Trump has consistently demonstrated that he's oddly drawn to people that don't mind getting on the wrong side of the law. Could Trump have perhaps learned that this woman once got herself arrested for shoplifting – while she held her three-month-old son in her arms? It just might have been that juicy tidbit that sealed the deal in Trump's demented mind, enabling this creature to slither right on down into his deep, dark wetlands.

<u>SWAMP DWELLER NUMBER EIGHTEEN</u>

- If there was ever a "communications" person who couldn't get her facts straight, this dweller is it! Just start with this quote of hers: "I can definitively say the president is not a liar, and I think it's frankly insulting that question would be asked."

- She also claimed the "president in no way form or fashion, has ever promoted or encouraged violence." Did she hope we'd believe she'd forgotten about the time Trump informed a group of law enforcement officers that they shouldn't be "too nice" to suspects? Although everyone is innocent until proven guilty in the United States, Trump had some advice for the police. He suggested that maybe they should take their hands away and not protect an individual's head – even when that person is struggling to get into the police car, with hands cuffed behind his back,!

- This dweller also pretended not to have noticed the occasions when Trump promoted violence at his rallies. During one of Trump's stump speeches, he trumpeted: "So if you see somebody getting ready to throw a tomato, knock the crap out of them, would you? I promise you, I will pay for the legal fees. I promise." At another of Trump's rallies, after security had ejected a protester, Trump proclaimed, "I'd like to punch him in the face."

- Further, this snake told reporters that Trump is only joking when he calls them the enemy of the people and encourages assault against them.

- In 2017, after Trump fired FBI Director James Comey, this dweller insisted that she: "heard from countless members of the FBI that are grateful and thankful for the president's decision." Emails from numerous FBI field office heads and prominent FBI officials proved otherwise.

- When the special counsel questioned this bog dweller, she admitted that her statement about Comey was a lie, describing it as a "slip of the tongue." Her tongue must have done an awful lot of slipping since she has repeated that false claim on countless occasions.

- This dweller admitted her statement about how the rank-and-file FBI agents had lost confidence in Comey wasn't founded on *anything*. She later tried to defend herself by stating that she had merely uttered such comments "in the heat of the moment."

- She also admitted to the special counsel that she had lied about the firing of Attorney General Jeff Sessions and Rod Rosenstein's connection to the firing of James Comey.

- This amphibious critter also claimed that Special Counsel Robert Mueller's report on Russian interference in the 2016 election decreed "a total and complete exoneration" of Trump. The summary of the report explicitly stated that it "does not exonerate him."

- This reptile denied that Trump dictated a fictitious statement about his son's Trump Tower meeting with Russians in 2016. Trump's own lawyers admitted that Trump had dictated that lie.

- When reporters asked this dweller to explain her inconsistent statements, she refused to answer, referring reporters back to the president's outside counsel. She also added, for our clarification, "I'm an honest person."

- Despite evidence and admissions to the contrary, this dweller denied that Trump paid hush money to the adult film star Stormy Daniels.

- This snake also insisted that immigrants who come to the United States through the diversity lottery system are not vetted. They *are*.

- She also incorrectly insisted that in 2016 President Barack Obama ordered the wiretapping of Trump's phones.

- After Trump accused Obama of such, this bottom-feeder spread another lie, claiming numerous mainstream news outlets had reported this to be true.

- This lying female dweller badmouthed the countless women who had accused Trump of sexual assault, condemning all of them as liars.

- After two ex-wives of a White House senior aide accused the aide of physical abuse, this dweller defended the man and claimed he is of "the highest integrity and exemplary character." She then deliberately obscured the details of how the White House had handled their investigation into these allegations. Eventually, when asked about this aide, she resorted to one of her typical template pacifiers: "The president supports victims of domestic violence and believes everyone should be treated fairly and with due process."

- This swamp dweller made countless conflicting and disproven statements about the aide accused of spousal abuse; she misrepresented information about his background checks and his eventual departure from the White House.

- After Trump retweeted doctored videos from a right-wing activist, designed to make us fear and hate Muslims, this dweller declared that it was perfectly fine for Trump to do so. "Whether it's a real video, the threat is real," she insisted.

- This snake, a mother of young children herself, never flinched when falsely claiming that laws that permit the separation of parents and their children at the border had been on the books for decades. She insisted those laws had forced the Trump administration to separate families and throw innocent children into cages.

- She accused Democrats of causing the entire human rights fiasco by refusing to close legal loopholes. Republicans were in charge at the time and had full power to close any such imagined loopholes. Though the Democrats were powerless in this issue, the dweller continually blamed them. The reality is that children were separated from their parents and thrown into cages because the Trump administration made border-crossing cases into criminal matters rather than civil ones.

- Many of the children in those detention centers, solely because of Trump's swamp policies, have suffered physical and sexual abuse. A reporter asked the dweller if she, as a parent of young children, had at least some empathy for these innocent kids. The dweller warned the reporter to "settle down." Then she accused him of grandstanding so he could get more time on air.

- She did some grandstanding herself (when questioned about how her boss had caused this humanitarian crisis) by stating that she thought it was "very biblical" to enforce the law. When a reporter pushed back on this absurd statement, the dweller proclaimed that she thought it must be very hard for that reporter to understand even short sentences.

- Numerous Christian leaders condemned these policies that came from Trump's swamp. One Bible scholar said the dweller's use of a biblical reference was a misuse of the Bible, similar to what slave traders and Nazis had done.

- While arguing for the need for Trump's wall, the dweller claimed that agents arrested 4,000 suspected terrorists as they tried to cross America's southern border. In actuality, during the time to which the dweller referred, the number of suspected terrorists encountered at Mexico's entry ports was *six*!

- It turns out those 4,000 terrorists had been apprehended at *airports*. Another convenient twisting of the truth? Or is this snake just not smart enough or informed enough to get her facts straight?

- This muddied creature claimed that in only one-and-one-half years, Trump created 700,000 new jobs for African Americans, adding that this was already more than the 195,000 jobs that President Obama had created for that demographic in *all of his eight years*. In reality, the Obama administration added approximately *three million* jobs for African Americans.

- After CNN's reporter Jim Acosta asked Trump a question that would prove embarrassing if Trump truthfully answered it, one of the swamp's interns, at Trump's direction, tried to snatch away the reporter's microphone. The reporter held on to it longer than Trump obviously desired. Later that day, Trump's swamp suspended Acosta's White House credentials.

- The next day the dweller, in an absurd attempt to justify the White House's highly criticized actions, released a video that a far right-wing conspiracy theorist had doctored. This altered video did not contain the part where Acosta said, "Pardon me, ma'am," to the intern. The phony visuals also made it appear as if the reporter had acted aggressively towards the female intern.

- The reptile claimed that Acosta had assaulted the woman and called his behavior "absolutely unacceptable."

- A slowed-down version of the *actual* video proved the dweller's claims were all BS.

- Acosta filed a lawsuit, which resulted in the swift reinstatement of his credentials.

- *The Washington Post* reported that this dweller, along with her deputy, strategized the perfect times to release announcements about revoking several of Trump's critics' security clearances. They intended for these declarations to distract from news cycles that proved uncomplimentary to Trump.

- At least twice, this snake violated federal law. When *The New York Times* published an op-ed that proved unfavorable to the Trump swamp, this dweller used her official government Twitter account to admonish the publication and give out the phone number of their opinion desk.

- After a restaurant co-owner refused to serve this snake, she used her official White House Twitter account against the restaurant. She even named the place, again violating ethics laws.

- This reptile resonates with Trump in more ways than just her compulsive lying. She enjoys taunting people about their perceived weaknesses or disabilities. During a Democratic presidential debate, this bottom-feeder mocked Joe Biden about his stutter, tweeting: *"I I I I I I I I I I I I I I I hhhave absolutely no idea what Biden is talking about."*

- If she wanted to protect her job, serving the most deceitful president in history, she had little choice but to be one of the most cunning and untrustworthy persons ever to hold her position. And this dweller embraced the task with unbounded enthusiasm. One opinion writer surmised that only a moral degenerate would have been capable of performing in the way she did.

- Taxpayers paid this dweller's salary to do her job and keep us informed about the Trump administration with truthfulness and precision. Trump tried justifying this dweller's multitude of lies in a tweet: "As a very active President with lots of things happening, it is not possible for my surrogates to stand at podium with perfect accuracy!"

- *Duh* . . . that was her *job* to be as accurate as possible. Taxpayers would likely even forgive a multitude of "imperfections" if they were unintended or at least well-intended. But this snake wouldn't even answer basic, legitimate questions. And taxpayers footed the bill for her salary while she repeatedly just made stuff up!

- Perhaps she *could* have been more accurate if she'd spent the minimum four hours each day that those who previously held her position had spent in preparing for formal briefings. Although taxpayers paid her well to keep Americans informed, this dweller often didn't even bother to brief reporters on anything. From time to time, at her convenience, she made herself available. You were most likely to hear from her when Trump needed someone to justify another pack of his lies.

- Instead of doing her job, as we paid her to do, this dweller circled the globe with Trump and enjoyed numerous side trip excursions. She jaunted off to go sightseeing at Buckingham Palace, took a sushi-making class in Tokyo, and became chummy with the Prince of Wales. While in Ireland, she visited Trump's private golf club and hung out in a local pub. She documented most of her little jaunts on Instagram so that all of us taxpayers (who footed the bill for her many vacations) could see the types of services she was providing for our country -- on our dime.

- As with many of Trump's swamp dwellers, this muddied creature slithered out from Trump's swamp and settled in another place – where she could continue to peddle her swampy talk: Fox News.

- As she departed Trump's marshland, she made it known that she hopes we will all remember her for her "transparency and honesty."

SWAMP DWELLER NUMBER NINETEEN

- This alligator doesn't dwell in the administration's main swamp. She hails from one of Trump's satellite locales – a vast landscape of grotty marshland. A place where Trump has made muddied, underwater landscapes of yuck and slime available to enrich his auxiliary team of gurgling swamp creatures. That wondrous land is otherwise known as – *Fox News*.

- Trump has been close to this alligator for over half a century. He knew her back in the days when this dweller was the district attorney of Westchester County, and her husband (who raised massive amounts of money for Republicans) was one of Trump's real estate lawyers.

- The dweller's husband allegedly came in handy when Trump needed someone to help him slice through New York City's zoning and land-use regulations.

- This soggy creature has joined Trump for Thanksgiving at Mar-a-Lago. She and her husband have jetted away with Trump on his private plane to savor lavish weekends in Palm Beach. Always eager to *jump for Trump*, the dweller herself described popping the movie popcorn on Trump's jet and heating Trump's meatloaf *at his request*.

- Several times this dweller has dined with Trump at the White House. She's threatened to "go straight to POTUS," if Trump's press aides declined her requests for interviews with Trump. She even warned them not to let Trump mention *any* other media personalities besides her in his speeches.

- This swamp vermin attempted to parlay all of her past *jumping for Trump* into a job in the Justice Department – a position that would have meant reporting to then Attorney General Jeff Sessions. Since this dweller lobbied so intensely for the spot, she clearly had no objection to working with Sessions. Trump interviewed her for the job, but, according to a senior administration official, Sessions blocked the appointment.

- Almost immediately after Sessions rejected her for the job, this dweller began attacking him on her TV show. Undoubtedly taking her cue from Trump's playbook, she chastised Sessions for recusing himself from the Russia investigation. The alligator referred to the man (that she'd lobbied so intensely to work for) as "the most dangerous man in America."

- Sources revealed that this dweller (who is just Trump's old friend and does not hold a sanctioned government position) met with Trump and discussed appointing a special counsel to investigate Hillary Clinton. After Sessions blocked that, this dweller and Trump facilitated a relentless campaign against the man, who had been one of Trump's closest friends and staunchest supporters.

- *Politico* revealed that this swampy organism petitioned Trump many times for the attorney general's job for herself, so perhaps she'd planned on pushing Sessions out all along, with or without Trump's help.

- Even after the duo successfully railroaded Sessions out of his position, Trump still did not invite this alligator to plunge into the White House swamp with the big fish. Trump realized this dweller would prove much more useful to him from the murky depths of his auxiliary swamp.

- Just because this alligator dwells offsite doesn't mean she can't lie for Trump every bit as quickly, and with the same stupefied absence of regret, as the crème de la crème of cold-blooded, corrupt reptiles who dwell in Trump's core White House swamp.

- From her platform as a television host, we have known this dweller for delivering blistering defenses of Trump. Various news sources have described her show as "almost universally positive about Trump," and "gushing." *Politico* observed: "From the outset of the administration, she has used her TV platform to hammer the president's critics and to ding his allies . . ."

- Trump's offsite swamp vermin has cried out to arrest anyone who cooperated with the special counsel's investigation into Russian meddling. She insisted that there should be a "cleansing" inside government agencies of any people deemed critical of Trump.

- She added that swamp bosses should not only fire such individuals but that they must be "taken out in cuffs."

- Trump's subservient dweller is a pro at "modifying" the truth to make Trump look good. She got wind of the fact that another dweller, Roger Stone, was planning on quitting Trump's campaign. On the night the network had scheduled Stone to appear on the alligator's TV show, Trump's little snitch quickly got word back to Trump of Stone's intentions. How loyal of her to provide Trump the opportunity (which he seized) to announce that he was *firing* his strategist before Stone had the chance to reveal his plans publicly.

- This alligator once proclaimed that President Obama released Abu Bakr al-Baghdadi, a notorious leader of ISIL. Not true. The *Bush* administration released that terrorist.

- The bottom-feeder described Democrats as hypocritical demons and "demon rats" while insisting that Brett Kavanaugh was the former altar boy they had crucified. She emphasized that Kavanaugh (whom multiple women have accused of various sexual misdeeds and who lived a wild and checkered past life) has "led the kind of exemplary life few of us can mirror."

- After Trump's response to the coronavirus left more than enough to be desired, this muddied creature declared that criticism of his handling of the outbreak was a conspiracy by the Democrats and the news media to undermine his reelection chances. She and a cohort at Fox News even claimed that those who criticized Trump's response were mere "panic pushers" who were inciting "mass hysteria."

- Although she publicly pedaled the theory that the coronavirus was merely an incitement of mass hysteria, that didn't stop her from endlessly hounding Trump's task force and FEMA officials until they sent 100,000 masks to the hospital of *her* choice.

- When two of Trump's senior swamp officials resigned after being accused of domestic abuse, this alligator suggested that Barack Obama's policies were to blame.

- In a similar demonstration of a lack of empathy towards sexually abused women, this reptile claimed the allegations of sexual abuse against Roger Ailes were "absurdities." She even attempted to get other women at Fox News to support that vile bully.

- After Trump blew his chance (while in Helsinki with Putin) to condemn Russia for their interference in the 2016 election, this dweller again came to Trump's defense. "What was he supposed to do, take a gun out and shoot Putin?"

- In a clear ethics violation, Trump posed for pictures with the dweller in the Oval Office to promote his old friend's book.

- This alligator spreads Trump's propaganda far and wide, even echoing Trump's talking points during parties at Mar-a-Lago.

- *Does anyone still remember the old days (before personalities like this muddied creature started manufacturing news for their own selfish purposes) when journalists reported what was actually happening?*

- Even the Trumpettes USA has given this dweller a starring role at some of their events. They're a group of dedicated, mostly female, Trump followers, whose mission statement is "making people, particularly women, aware of what a great president and savior of our country, Donald J. Trump will be."

- Trump's old friend declared to the Trumpettes: "This man (Trump) is a genius – he's not unstable – he's a damn genius." Not only did she promote her old friend, but, against all ethical codes, she helped drop substantial money into Trump's pocket.

- The dweller declared Trump our victorious hero, for making it possible for us to utter *Merry Christmas* once again.

- This alligator once described Trump as "almost superhuman."

- This woman is dangerous; she knows exactly how to connect with and manipulate Trump's hard-core base. The dweller advised her listeners: "Get a gun, buy one legally, learn how to shoot it, and be primed to use it. And, I don't care if you get a long gun, a handgun, a revolver or a semi-automatic. Get whatever gun you can handle, and don't let anyone talk you out of it."

- She's also criticized one of Trump's favorite targets, Representative Ilhan Omar. She claimed that Omar's wearing of the traditional hijab signaled that the congresswoman was more loyal to Sharia law than to the U.S. Constitution.

- After that disingenuous racist statement, the dweller's show lost sponsors. Even the heads at Fox News took notice and suspended Trump's alligator for a few weeks.

- Trump started fuming when he tuned in to one of his favorite TV shows, and his servant alligator didn't immediately pop onto his screen to overindulge his voracious cravings for dripping adoration. Absent also was this dweller's mealy-mouthed attempts at spinning Trump's alternative "facts."

- Like a spoiled brat, whining to her overindulgent daddy, this swampy organism raced straight to Trump and insisted that he get her back on the air, pronto! Trump called the head of Fox News and demanded the network reinstate his swamp creature.

- Trump (who evidently has nothing better to do than maintain absolute control over his entire empire of swampland) also madly tweeted for his dweller's return. In his tweets, he instructed Fox News to "stay true to the people that got you there." He continued to ramble on about things that had zero connection to why they had suspended his alligator, such as "radical left Democrats" and the "fake news media." He kept up the pressure until Fox returned his lying alligator to the airwaves, and she resumed her previously scheduled ritual of stroking Trump.

- We all know by now how Trump loves his fast driving, drunken cohorts. This swamp creature once revealed that her biggest pet peeve was people who "drive slow in the passing lane." She often mentions cars, including her first car, which was the color "British Racing Green."

- The police once clocked her racing through upstate New York at 119 miles per hour.

- On one episode of her show, that she had hosted from home because of the pandemic, someone had to cover for her for the first fifteen minutes citing "technical difficulties." After the dweller finally appeared on-air, she seemed to be disheveled and was slurring her speech. Social media erupted with speculation that she was drunk out of her skull. Viewers even spotted her quickly trying to hide a drink with a straw in it after returning from a commercial break.

- They say you're known by the company you keep. This alligator's husband (who was also part of Trump's previous swamp life) is no prize either. The man allegedly has mob connections.

- He fathered a daughter with another woman while married to Trump's alligator.

- Throughout extensive court hearings, he denied the child was his. He even claimed the mother was trying to extort him and accused her of being mentally unstable.

- Kind of stupid, *hey*, in these days of DNA?

- The DNA test proved our dweller's husband to be the liar.

- Conclusive tests didn't even stop this deceitful man from hiring a private detective to try to dig up dirt on the woman that he'd made love to, at least once. And, just like most of Trump's swampy cronies, the lying man deducted the cost of that investigation as a business expense on his taxes.

- It's people like this unscrupulous man, (who are always sniffing out ways to stiff the United States Treasury), that force the rest of us to foot the bill. But that wasn't his only crime. A jury agreed he was a crook when they found him guilty of 34 charges, including conspiracy, tax evasion, and 28 counts of filing a false tax return.

- Trump's alligator (district attorney at the time) criticized the investigation as "invasive and hostile." She also claimed that any matters the prosecutors brought up that involved her were "a desperate attempt by them to bring me into this wherever they can." Did she not consider that perhaps the prosecutors brought up the fact that the dweller's lying husband declared a Mercedes for his wife and one for his mother as a business deduction merely because her husband's actions were . . . *illegal*? And that the prosecutors were only doing their *jobs*?

- One of our dwellers' former secretaries testified that this alligator regularly forwarded her personal bills to her husband's business for payment. She also co-signed numerous fraudulent tax returns.

- For such an extensive list of convictions, the reptile's husband didn't serve very much time in prison. And upon his release, our dweller took him right back.

- Though her husband's legion of financial crimes clearly didn't bother our dweller one bit, her reaction was quite different when she suspected he was cheating on her again. She went to Bernie Kerik, a former New York City police commissioner, and asked him to bug her husband's boat. Kerik was under investigation himself for tax fraud, ethics violations, and making false statements. Federal agents were secretly recording him. The dweller soon found herself under investigation for possible illegal wiretapping. Like her current-day swamp boss loves to do, she accused federal agents of a "political witch hunt."

- Though Trump has not yet invited this alligator to slither and slosh through his core wastelands, make no mistake – being a fixer for Trump from the auxiliary bog has proven quite lucrative for this dweller. She now earns big bucks for giving speeches to conservative Republican groups.

- The day after one such campaign speech for Kevin McCarthy, the minority leader appeared on the dweller's show. Together they lauded Trump's efforts to "drain the swamp." McCarthy added it was necessary because "you can't trust what's happening."

<u>**SWAMP DWELLER NUMBER TWENTY**</u>

- Before entering Trump's official swamp, this dweller was a Fox News executive. But, no doubt to save face, the network got rid of this alligator.

- After filing sexual harassment complaints against Roger Ailes, several women had accused this dweller of working to silence them and enabling Ailes' behavior. One female Fox host claimed this dweller told her: "Don't fight this."

- Many have stated that this dweller knew that the network had hired private detectives to intimidate the alleged victims of Roger Ailes.

- This alligator was subpoenaed in a criminal investigation into the misuse of funds over at Fox. Investigators believed he covered for Ailes when his boss used company monies to silence women he had sexually harassed and abused.

- According to one of Ailes' blackmailed victims, this reptile worked extra hard to ensure that she wouldn't talk. He monitored her e-mails, checking to see if she was saying anything negative about Ailes. While Fox executives had this woman sequestered at a New York hotel, this alligator, in true cult fashion, reviewed all of her external communications, including those with her family.

- He arranged for this woman to see a psychiatrist, one that he had personally obtained. That psychiatrist kept her heavily medicated and eventually hospitalized her.

- Another of Ailes' victims also alleged that this alligator led Fox's campaign to monitor her private "phone and email communications." She claimed their goal was to "intimidate, terrorize, and crush her through an endless stream of lewd, offensive, and career-damaging social media posts, blog entries, and commentary."

- This former Fox News host provided email evidence that the dweller used an outside social media firm to use "sock puppets" against her and anyone else that criticized the Fox network.

Creating false social media accounts to manipulate public opinion is a criminal violation.

- Reports surfaced that this amphibious critter also knew that Ailes used private investigators to bully and intimidate journalists.

- A lawsuit alleged this alligator sent investigators and lawyers to badger a man's friends, customers, neighbors, and family to uncover potentially damaging information. He then used "sock puppet" media postings to out the man as being gay.

- Fox News did ask this dweller to leave, yet they awarded him with around $15 million on the way out. They continued to pay him while he worked for the Trump Swamp, raising numerous ethics issues.

- This reptile had zero personal experience in dealing with the press when Trump first considered his resume.

- In spite of, or *because of*, the man's lack of experience and unscrupulous ways, Trump hired this reptile to be the White House deputy chief of staff for communications; he also named him as an assistant to the president. According to people familiar with the situation, Trump's close friend at Fox News, Sean Hannity, helped persuade Trump to hire this bottom-feeder.

- Usually, the person in this dweller's communications position works hard to keep the taxpayers correctly informed about what's going on in their country. But this alligator's job was to make Trump look good on TV.

- Trump clearly liked the fact that this swamp creature had an excellent sense of stagecraft. For Trump's unveiling of Kavanaugh, his Supreme Court nominee, this creature in Trump's black lagoon knew precisely how to take advantage of the East Room's warm cream colors, with its glimmering floors, low-hanging chandeliers, and golden swaged drapes. He toyed with the podium's position, the backdrop, the microphone's height, and the camera angles. He brought in extra stage lights and tweaked the illumination until he finally tricked Trump into believing that all those efforts actually made him look good.

- This reptile also helped put together "gorgeous" videos of Trump in the Rose Garden, all on the taxpayers' dime, of course.

- They say you're known by the company you keep. This dweller's wife has a history of defending racists and has posted numerous racially charged comments on Twitter. She's also ranted on social media about countless other controversial subjects such as "Islamic Insanity," and she's promoted unfounded anti-vaccination conspiracies. She stealthily deleted her Twitter account as soon as the White House cleared her husband to dive into Trump's swamp.

- One of this dweller's first swamp "tasks" was blocking a reporter from attending an open press event in the Rose Garden. Her only "crime" had been embarrassing Trump by calling out a few pertinent questions.

- After several unfriendly encounters with reporters himself, this muddied creature ended up steering Trump towards "friendlier" interviews at Fox News.

- Before very long, Trump realized he had enough of his own connections over at Fox. He sent this dweller (like countless snakes, alligators, and other assorted reptiles before and after) on his merry way.

CHAPTER FIVE-
MIXIN' IT UP

Trump loves to mingle with all sorts of seedy characters. Sometimes their unsavory personalities are the only common threads that bind them. Let's have some fun in this chapter (*and make it a little harder to guess who's who?*) by mixing up our dwellers a bit.

SWAMP DWELLER NUMBER TWENTY-ONE

- Before his time in Trump's swamp, this dweller spent two years languishing in another quagmire. He served as chief of staff to a former Florida lieutenant governor who was forced to resign. This lieutenant governor had done consulting work for a phony veteran's charity. Prosecutors said this scam laundered over $300 million from illegal gambling parlors.

- According to a political consulting firm's website, where this dweller also worked before his days in Trump's White House swamp, this alligator "worked on the ground tirelessly to help President Trump win Florida." Subsequently, Trump readily uncovered a place of honor in the sludge for this man whose only "qualification" was that he'd worked on his campaign.

- The alligator didn't have any education needed for the crucial public affairs position appointed to him inside the Environmental Protection Agency (EPA). He didn't even have a background in science or the environment, yet the swamp bosses put him in charge of reviewing every award the agency gives out. The reptile had the last word on hundreds of millions of dollars in funding decisions for all the grants the EPA distributes.

- While it's highly unusual for a political operative to override scientific experts' recommendations, this dweller made a swamp specialty out of bucking the scientific community.

- Agency employees claimed this soggy creature told staff that he is on guard for "the double C-word" – his reference to climate change when he reviews grant applications. Reportedly, he continually instructed grant officers to eliminate all references to climate change in solicitations.

- This alligator rescinded pre-approved funding to causes that would have proven beneficial to our environment and eliminated grants that could have helped lessen some of the impacts of the world's climate crisis.

- Besides eradicating that *nasty* double C-word, this dweller endangered our environment even further by playing dirty politics. He took definite aim at Obama administration priorities.

- He also cut back grant awards to numerous democratic-leaning states. But this dweller put everyone's interests, from every political party, at risk *if* they didn't immediately hitch a ride on the Trump train. On the *same day* that Republican Senator Lisa Murkowski of Alaska voted against a GOP health-care bill, the EPA halted grants to the regional office that covers Alaska.

- Besides siphoning a lucrative salary for himself, Trump's swamp granted this bottom-feeder permission to moonlight for private clients. Though the swamp provided Congress with a copy of their permission letter, they deliberately blacked out this swamp creature's clients' names.

- House Democrats sent a letter of protest to this alligator's boss. The message read: "A political appointee cutting millions of dollars in funding to EPA grant recipients on what appears to be a politically motivated basis, while at the same time being authorized to serve as a paid media consultant to unnamed outside clients, raises serious concerns of potential conflicts of interest."

- Apparently, no one deemed the letter worthy enough to warrant a response.

SWAMP DWELLER NUMBER TWENTY-TWO

- While working at SpiritBank, this lizard granted another swamp creature (who ended up becoming his boss in Trump's swamp) at least three home mortgages that the second dweller seemed incapable of paying back.

- This reptile also lent money to this other swamp creature's partnership so that they could acquire a minor league baseball team.

- The Federal Deposit Insurance Corporation (FDIC) concluded that this lizard had proven his "unfitness to serve" or even participate in the conduct of a bank.

- The FDIC even barred him from engaging in any other banking duties!

- Despite the man having zero qualifications for the position, or maybe *because of* his unsavory background, Trump picked this reptile to run the EPA's Superfund program for cleaning up highly hazardous waste.

- In keeping with the usual fashion of conflicts of interest in Trump's bog, this dweller owns stock in a company responsible for significant contamination to our environment.

<u>SWAMP DWELLER NUMBER TWENTY-THREE</u>

- Here's a guy – a shrewd businessman from Chile – who knows exactly how to get what he wants. When he needs a special favor, he looks for the people who would be instrumental in awarding him whatever it is he desires at the moment. He finds out what these people need, then figures out how to grant them their every longing. After which . . . *he zooms in for the payoff.*

- This dweller has the money to sponsor his every quid pro quo whim. His family is the wealthiest in all of Chile, with *Forbes* valuing the family's industrial, banking, and mining empire at over $13 *billion*!

- In his home country, citizens claimed that this businessman attempted to win favor with a Chilean president's family. A bank that this reptile controls approved a $10 million loan for these family members, but only *after* the election when they could prove useful.

- All parties involved denied anything inappropriate occurred.

- These days this billionaire wants to bring sulfide-ore copper mining to Minnesota. The area he set his sights on is a rich habitat – home to thousands of animal species, including the Canada lynx and the gray wolf.

- But this muddied life form doesn't give a crap about animals. The dollar signs in his eyes have also blinded him to the majestic beauty of this pristine wilderness. He only sees what he believes lies below the surface – tons of copper and nickel ore – an estimated $40 *billion* in minerals.

- When exposed to water or oxygen, the ore generates toxic sulfuric acid, which would likely pollute the nearby water system. The dweller's planned mine in Minnesota's Rainy River watershed would drain into the protected Boundary Waters wilderness area.

- Thomas Tidwell, former chief of the United States Forest Service, said after a 2016 analysis that mining this vast landscape of federally protected forests and lakes could easily cause the leaching of harmful metals into the waters. He concluded this venture would risk: "serious and irreplaceable harm to this unique, iconic, and irreplaceable wilderness area."

- Despite this dweller's firm spending $160,000 lobbying Congress, the Obama administration recognized that the proposed mine would bring with it an exorbitant degree of environmental risk and opted to save this natural area by halting this alligator's plans.

- Our Chilean reptile immediately sued the Federal Government claiming through a company statement that Obama's move would "hinder access to one of the world's largest sources of copper, nickel, and platinum – resources of strategic importance to the U.S. economy and national defense."

Comforting, hey – to learn a billionaire from a foreign country frets away his days and nights in his Chilean mansion worrying about America's resources and defenses!

- But this alligator wasn't able to sink his claws into any precious American soil under the Obama administration. Since 1926 the U.S. has recognized the importance of this area. The government has protected this 1.1-million-acre landscape of lakes and forest that partially sits on U.S. Forest Service land, next to the Boundary Waters Canoe Area Wilderness.

But suddenly, one day it started to look as if Trump might actually win the election . . .

The dweller's wheels started spinning . . .

Perhaps an opening – a chance to finally destroy one of America's last pristine and wondrous natural areas in this dweller's quest to pilfer American resources.

- Just like back in Chile, this muddied creature waited to make his move until *after* Trump secured the election. The Trump entourage was just starting to roll into D.C., and it became known that Trump's privileged daughter and her crooked husband were searching for that perfect house to rent. *Coincidentally,* our dweller purchased what turned out to be the couple's dream home – a $5.5 million mansion in Washington, D.C. The dweller's real estate agents lined up Ivanka Trump and Jared Kushner to rent this place from him before this bottom-feeder even took possession of the house.

- There are conflicting opinions as to whether Trump's family is getting a real bargain rental or not. But a house that this couple really wanted suddenly became available to them, and at a price that was lower than they had discussed paying elsewhere. Several real estate experts have surmised that the landlord is more-than-likely losing out (financially) on this residential deal.

- With the "kiddies" happily tucked away in the Chilean billionaire's D.C. mansion, Trump immediately went to work on his daughter's landlord's *problem*. According to obtained government calendars and e-mails, senior Trump officials, including the White House's top energy adviser, almost immediately discussed the project with the dweller's mining company.

- Swamp dwellers marked communications related to the project TIME SENSITIVE. They quickly began removing roadblocks to the proposed mine, ignoring all concerns that this mine could harm the Boundary Waters, more than a *million* acres of federally protected lakes and forests along the Canadian border. Even before the administration appointed an interior secretary, swamp dwellers reexamined and eventually restored leases for this mine.

- Trump's agriculture secretary assured Congress there would be an extensive environmental review. But the Forest Service (the same agency that had concluded that the mining would risk: "serious and irreplaceable harm to this unique, iconic, and irreplaceable wilderness area," suddenly halted all reviews, insisting that neither a ban or even a study was necessary.

- The rush of activities and the keen focus on this otherwise little-known Minnesota project, which had not played a part in Trump's campaign, astonished numerous department officials from previous administrations.

- Representative Raúl M. Grijalva, Chairman of the House Natural Resources Committee, stated that the Trump administration "blatantly ignored scientific and economic evidence" in their decision making. He also felt that the company's owner, renting a house to Trump's family members, was an "interesting coincidence."

- Neither the White House nor Trump's family cared to confirm if ethics officials had reviewed the rental deal. But, just as happened back in Chile, all parties involved denied anything inappropriate occurred.

- We could *almost* believe this situation was legit. The reptile explained that he bought up a few D.C. properties because wealthy people from a new administration would be making their way into town, which could mean big bucks for this dweller. And possibly, the Trump administration's rush to push the project through could merely stem from Trump's usual disdain for the natural world and his unquenched desire to cater to big business. Also, Trump wants to create as many jobs as possible (whatever the quality or safety of those jobs, and whatever the ultimate cost to our country) so he can curry favor with the voters that he relies on to allow him to keep pretending to be king. This project *would* create jobs. A handful of locals are even in favor of the mine.

- But while we could *almost* start believing this was all just a coincidence (as Trump's soggy swamp creature would have us think), certain questions come to mind: Didn't this alligator do nearly the same thing back in his home country with the Chilean president's family? If he *had* purchased the D.C. mansion just to make money by renting the place – why have so many experts claimed that this dweller is losing money on this deal? Why hadn't he listed the mansion for rent on the Metropolitan Regional Information System, which advertises such listings? And why would this dweller feel it necessary to obscure his identity as Ivanka and Jared's landlord by hiding behind a listing company he'd named on the deed?

- In Chile, environmental groups raised serious concerns because of the dweller's mining company's toxic spills. This bottom-feeder's organization played down all those claims, even declaring that it was "proud" of its environmental record.

- Trump didn't believe in "wasting" any time by examining the mining company's safety record before he rushed to hand this billionaire the keys to America's Kingdom. Maybe after this guy from Chile transforms America's pristine lakes and forests into additional toxic swampland, it will provide Trump and his myriad of swamp creatures with extra room to spread out. They would never refuse some additional, fresh, new swampy playgrounds.

- As long as Jared and Ivanka, and all of Trump's family and cohorts get to experience *their* American dreams, they expect the working-class people to rest *quietly* (unless screaming out in adoration of the phony king) and savor the notion that Trump is putting AMERICA FIRST!

U.S.A.! U.S.A.! FOUR MORE YEARS! FOUR MORE YEARS! – RAISED FIST, RIGHT ARM, HIGH FIVE, FISTBUMP! U.S.A! U.S.A!

U.S.A.! U.S.A.! FOUR MORE YEARS! FOUR MORE YEARS! – RAISED FIST, RIGHT ARM, HIGH FIVE, FISTBUMP! U.S.A! U.S.A!

Now that's what I'm talkin' about!

<u>SWAMP DWELLER NUMBER TWENTY-FOUR</u>

- When President Obama suggested eliminating the carried interest rate – an unfair tax loophole that made this dweller super-rich – this reptile ranted that Obama's endeavors were like "when Hitler invaded Poland in 1939."

- This snake is the founder, chairman, and CEO of an organization (The Blackstone Group) that has been cited for utilizing similar unfair tax advantages in the U.K.

- This reptile did not immediately support Trump – until he realized he'd be able to mold Trump to his way of thinking when it comes to taxes.

- Though the dweller compared Obama's desires to help the American working class to Hitler's unspeakable attrocities, this swampy organism stated that people had unfairly criticized Trump when he failed to denounce neo-Nazis.

- This dweller donated $27 million in 2020 alone to Republican politicians.

- This snake put Mitch McConnell's billionaire brother-in-law on the board of his company. This reptile also donated at least $8 million to McConnell's Super PAC.

- Employees of the dweller's company have donated over $10 million to McConnell's Super PAC.

- The snake donated $5.5 million to Republicans during the election cycle. He also donated $850,000 to Trump's inauguration and political action committees.

- Blackstone's real estate division did business with Jared Kushner, lending Kushner's family business and their partners $312 million.

- This dweller loves throwing lavish parties, especially for himself. Reporters estimated the costs of his birthday celebrations at $10 million to $20 million each. These costs are chump change for him after all the extra money he took in by working those tax loopholes and manipulating Trump. Working-class people, who play by the rules, make up the slack for slimy snakes like him.

Because of this dweller, many of those hard-working people can't even afford to order a pizza for *their children's* birthday parties.

- The dweller hosted a $100,000 per plate fundraiser for Trump as the GOP debated details of the upcoming tax cut. Attendees made "suggestions" to Trump about the proposed legislation. Days later, Trump adjusted the tax proposal in their favor.

- Though Trump had criticized the carried interest rate on many occasions (repeatedly slamming it during his campaign and claiming people who benefited from it were getting away with murder), the Swamp King has made zero effort to close this dweller's beloved loophole.

- The reptile's organization, Blackstone, has been accused of exploitation and disenfranchisement of vulnerable people across the globe.

- Blackstone engages in shadow banking. They lend money, but they're not technically a bank – so they're not mandated to abide by banking regulations.

- The dweller's organization has lobbied congress to have American employers invest 3 percent of an employee's salary into retirement products that *they* sell. They want to siphon off a share of the profits by charging exorbitant fees, thus taking more money out of the pockets of the working class.

- After the housing crash, Blackstone bought up a ton of foreclosed homes. The Blackstone Group is now the largest owner of single-family rental homes in the country.

- Many have observed that The Blackstone Group managed these homes more as a slumlord than a landlord. They left homes in disrepair and shifted the responsibility of maintenance to the tenants. Requests to fix electrical and plumbing issues went directly to voicemail and remained unanswered.

- They hit tenants with sudden, unreasonable eviction notices. At least one warning came even after Blackstone's own system was at fault for failing to report a rent payment. Other times, they sent eviction notices for non-payment before the rent was due.

- Even officials in Denmark complained that the firm had pushed people out of their homes, to assure fast returns on its investments.

- Representatives from the United Nations Housing Division and the U.N. Working Group on Business and Human Rights criticized Blackstone, stating that its business practices (frequent rent increases and forceful evictions) contributed to the global housing crisis.

- This bottom-feeder's company is also helping to perpetuate the global climate crisis.

- Blackstone owns a significant share in Hidrovias, a Brazilian company that operates in and around the Amazon rainforest. This company has cleared hundreds of miles of the rainforest for a highway that leads to its export terminal.

- The move itself has not only demolished vast sections of the rainforest, but the company's exports have also incentivized farmers to cultivate the land to grow grains and soy for short-term profits. Many are burning their way through the forest to acquire these lands. Experts estimate there were over 70,000 intentionally set fires in the Amazon rainforest in less than one year.

- If deforestation continues, the Amazon will just collapse on its own as its natural water recycling pump will become too weak to maintain the system. The climate crisis will be fast-tracked and civilization as we know it will be altered forever.

- This dweller has been generous with a portion of his money, but his donations always come with *stipulations*.

- Like Trump, he loves seeing his name on buildings. In return for his donation to his old high school, he wanted the school renamed after him. He insisted that school leaders prominently display a portrait of himself inside and name other parts of the campus after his brothers, track coach, and some of his old buddies from the track team.

- This snake also wanted input in constructing the new campus, reserving the right to have all contractors approved by him. He even insisted on timely reports on the progress of the school's computer literacy program. Showing no signs of slowing down, he also wanted to change the school's curriculum, requiring that students take specific courses that HE picked for them. Unless the dweller himself allowed any details of the deal to be released, he insisted everything about the agreement had to be *hush-hush*.

- After making a large donation to New York City's public library, the dweller insisted they display his name "at a minimum" in the building's front and above each of the entrances.

- It's never an agreeable undertaking to carve up a landmark structure. New York's Landmarks Preservation Commission must approve any alterations to the building, such as new inscriptions.

- This beautiful ornate building also features the names of John Jacob Astor, James Lenox, and Samuel Tilden. Their contributions helped build the library in the first place – yet each of their names is only displayed once.

- Library officials got so frustrated with the dweller's demands, one of them sarcastically suggested carving the reptile's name into the roof. That way, passengers on every passing plane could avail themselves of the glorious sight!

- This bog dweller has become one of Trump's biggest donors.

- Trump gave the swampy creature a position as chair of the Strategic and Policy Forum, which Trump disbanded to save face, after members began to quit.

- Though this reptile does not hold an actual governmental position in the administration's swamp, he maintains rare and regular access to Trump as one of his key advisers.

- The dweller owns an opulent home just down the road from Trump's Mar-a-Lago, and the two men often meet privately.

- Although the dweller has numerous conflicts of interest, many of them in China, Trump consults with this reptile on his negotiations with China.

- Trump refers to this dweller as his "China Whisperer."

- This amphibious critter and Trump held a private meeting at the Davos summit. During a subsequent panel discussion, the reptile praised Trump's handling of the economy, adding: "It's a time of enormous ebullience. You are making money, and it is really not hard."

- Tell that to the hardworking parents, struggling to throw their kids any kind of birthday party at all. These parents might be able to provide their children with a night to remember if *their* tax money wasn't being diverted to help pay for this dweller's lavish celebrations! But eliminating even a few seconds of this snake's dazzling fireworks displays – to pay for a few hundred birthday pizzas, for a few hundred hopeful kids, would (according to Trump's dweller) be akin to the worst atrocities that Hitler ever inflicted upon the human race.

SWAMP DWELLER NUMBER TWENTY-FIVE

- Though the George W. Bush administration vetted this dweller for a position, they ultimately passed on hiring this lizard.

- Trump offered this bottom-feeder the position he had sought for years, at nearly double the usual salary.

- After much scrutiny, the swamp creature agreed to lower his salary expectations.

- During the AIDS epidemic in the 1980s and 1990s, this dweller was an Army major working at Walter Reed Medical Institute.

- This lizard insisted on mandatory testing of all troops for AIDS, without providing confidentiality.

- He aggressively investigated the pasts of any army personnel who tested positive. You could often find him rummaging through their personal belongings, searching for signs of homosexuality.

- He designed policies which quarantined those infected with AIDS in a special barracks known as the *HIV Hotel* or the *Leper Colony*.

- The reptile humiliated soldiers before having them discharged and left to die of the disease.

- Most of those he ousted died impoverished and without medical insurance. Many of them committed suicide.

- This dweller wrote the introduction to the book "Christians in the Age of AIDS."

- He worked closely with a group that maintained that AIDS was "God's judgment" against homosexuals. He called out to reject *anyone* that he felt wanted to replace God as a judge.

- This bottom-feeder condemned distributing condoms to sexually active adults.

- He has described anti-discrimination programs as efforts of "false prophets."

- The dweller backed a House bill that would have subjected people to HIV testing and subsequent loss of professional licenses along with forced quarantine.

- This muddied creature backed a potential AIDS vaccine while appearing to misrepresent the data, which caused the Army to investigate him for scientific misconduct.

- The Army acknowledged there were issues concerning the accuracy of the dweller's data but eventually cleared him of the allegations of intentional wrongdoing.

- Even after the Army gave him the benefit of the doubt, stating it was possible he had potentially made some *innocent mistakes*, the dweller continued to support the vaccine, even pushing for Congress to fund a $20 million clinical trial.

- Ultimately, that vaccine never worked.

- Currently, (as of October 2020), the dweller sits on Trump's Coronavirus Task Force. We are counting on him to keep us safe during the pandemic.

- Nearly every medical expert has warned that much more testing must be done before a potential coronavirus vaccine can safely and effectively be made available to the public. Even the vaccine companies themselves put out a letter stating that they will not make a vaccine available until all these mandatory precautions have been taken.

- Despite these warnings, this dweller sent a letter (an urgent request) to the nation's governors. He stated that the Trump swamp wants them to do everything humanly possible to eliminate any hurdles in making vaccine distribution sites fully operational in their states – even if this means waiving requirements and fast-tracking permits and licenses. By when does this bottom-feeder insist all the states be ready for Trump's swamp to roll out their vaccine? You guessed it – two days before Election Day!

CHAPTER SIX

BONUS ROUND

Need some extra points? Figure out who the dweller is in these additional credit rounds and give yourself *ten* extra points for each correct answer!

<u>BONUS ROUND EXTRA CREDIT DWELLER NUMBER ONE</u>

In May 2016, in the well-heeled neighborhood of West London, this dweller made his way into a classy wine bar to meet with Australia's High Commissioner to the U.K., Alexander Downer.

We all know how Trump loves his drunks, and loose lips sink ships, so here comes another alleged drunken incident. This dweller was a foreign policy adviser to the Trump campaign at the time of his meeting with Downer. The two men supposedly ordered vodkas (in a wine bar) though how many each man consumed is anyone's guess.

While the alcohol was flowing, the alligator allegedly told Australia's top diplomat in Britain all about how Russia was attempting to discredit Hillary Clinton and had hacked thousands of her emails.

Months later, when hacked emails from Democrats were made public, Australian officials passed on the particulars about the dweller's meeting with Downer to U.S. intelligence. This information was at least part of the reason for opening the investigation into the Trump campaign's ties to Russia.

This dweller claims he never said a word about the stolen emails to Downer, but admitted that weeks before the meeting, he did learn that Moscow had thousands of Clinton's emails that they'd hacked with the intention of harming her campaign.

The dweller even admitted to telling Greece's Foreign Minister all about the e-mails! It makes you wonder what this alligator might have been guzzling on *that* occasion!

The bottom-feeder also pleaded guilty to lying to Robert Mueller about the emails.

Overall, the documented recollections of both of these men of their meeting at that posh wine bar on that fateful, rainy night, were surprisingly similar. And interestingly enough . . . neither man would admit to having had *too* much to drink. But there remains a crucial difference in their stories . . .

Did Trump's alligator actually spill his guts about Clinton's e-mails? If not, just how *did* the Australian diplomat learn about them? Downer reported the possible existence of those hacked emails to Australian Intelligence right after he met with Trump's bottom-feeder. That was *months* before any information about those e-mails became public.

<u>BONUS ROUND EXTRA CREDIT DWELLER NUMBER TWO</u>

This high-ranking lowlife, who has immense influence in Trump's sinkhole, attended a coronavirus briefing in late January 2020. Health and Human Services Secretary, Alex Azar, presented the newest virus news and attempted to get this bottom-feeder to focus on the extreme dangers of the disease and the potential for impending disaster. Showing zero concern over a deadly pandemic about to invade our shores, this creature from the black lagoon completely shifted the subject.

He instead badgered Azar about the swamp's "messy decision" to implement a partial ban on flavored e-cigarettes. "Why did you push me to insert myself into a controversial political issue?" this reptile demanded of Azar.

This dweller's ignorance and indifference assuredly precipitated the senseless deaths of tens of thousands of Americans.

CHAPTER SEVEN –

IDENTIFY THAT DWELLER

IDENTITIES FROM CHAPTER ONE –
CROOKED CABINET

1. Elaine Chao, Secretary of Transportation

2. Betsy Devos, Secretary of Education

3. Ben Carson, Secretary of Housing and Urban Development

4. Steve Mnuchin, Secretary of the Treasury

5. Wilbur Ross, Secretary of Commerce

6. Rudy Giuliani, personal attorney to Donald J. Trump

7. Sam Nunberg, former political advisor to the Trump Campaign

8. Vince Vaughn, actor, producer, screenwriter, comedian

9. Stephanie Grisham, White House official, former Press Secretary, and Communications Director

10. Larry Kudlow, Director of National Economic Council

IDENTITIES FROM CHAPTER THREE –
WHILE WE'RE ON THE SUBJECT – A FEW MORE
DRUNKS

11. Corey Lewandowski, former Trump Campaign Manager

12. Max Miller, Deputy Campaign Manager

13. Ronny Jackson, former physician to the Swamp King

14. Kevin Chmielewski, former Deputy Chief of Staff for Operations at the EPA

15. Andrew Puzder, nominee for Secretary of Labor

IDENTITIES FROM CHAPTER FOUR – COMMUNICATIONS REPTILES

16. Anthony Scaramucci, former White House Communications Director

17. Katrina Pierson, Senior Adviser to the Trump Campaign, former National Spokesperson for the Trump Campaign

18. Sarah Huckabee Sanders, former White House Press Secretary

19. Jeanine Pirro, Fox News television host

20. Bill Shine, former Deputy Chief of Staff for Communications

21. John Konkus, former Deputy Associate Administrator, EPA

22. Albert "Kell" Kelly, Former Senior Adviser to Administrator, EPA

23. Andrónico Luksic, Chilean businessman

24. Stephen A. Schwarzman, businessman, investor, and philanthropist.

25. Robert Redfield, Director of the CDC

IDENTITIES FROM CHAPTER SIX – BONUS ROUND

Extra Credit Dweller Number One

George Papadopoulos, former member of Trump's Foreign Policy Advisory Panel

Extra Credit Dweller Number Two

Donald J. Trump, Swamp Master

WHAT YOUR SCORE MEANS

91 - 120

Wow! You're amazing! The best. Congratulations. And thanks for the support in reading my book, though you really didn't need to. You should have *written* it. Let me know if you want to contribute to my next edition.

81 - 90

You know a lot. Some might say you're *too* tightly wound. Take a break from politics. Get out and enjoy life (practicing social distancing, of course) and wait for my next book. Remember, Karen Ann Carpenter scrutinizes the news, so you don't have to.

71 - 80

Congratulations. You know more about what's happening in America than the average person. But maybe you know a bit too much. Consider taking a break from politics and waiting for my next book. Remember, Karen Ann Carpenter scrutinizes the news, so you don't have to.

61 - 70

Congratulations. You're keeping your eyes open. No one in America is pulling the wool over your eyes. We need more people like you. Very nice!

51 - 60

Congratulations. You show a balanced mixture of being aware of what's going on in America, but you still take time to smell the roses. Nice! Keep up those keen observations.

41 - 50

Congratulations. You know what's going on. You also don't appear to get overly obsessed with politics. Nice! Hopefully, this book helped fill in some of the gaps you might have had.

31 - 40

Congratulations. You've been paying some attention. But maybe you want to listen up just a little more often?

21 - 30

Congratulations on finishing this book. You needed it. I hope it's been helpful, and you plan on keeping an eye on the crooks that are running our world more closely from now on. If not, never fear. Just wait for my next book. Remember, Karen Ann Carpenter scrutinizes the news, so you don't have to.

11- 20

Get your head out of your computer games and stop yakking it up with your BFF's, or stop doing whatever you do all day that wastes so much time. You need to pay attention to what's happening in America. All of our futures are at stake.

0 - 10

Let me know when you get back from Mars. I'll send you a copy of my latest book. You're going to need it.

SOURCES

@RealDonaldTrump

ABC News

ABCNews.go.com

AJC.com

Anchorage Daily News

ATF.gov

AviationDaily.news

Aviation.travel

AZCapitolTimes.com

Ballotpedia.org

BBC.com

BipartisanReport.com

Bloomberg.com

Buffalo News

Business Insider

CNN

CommonDreams.org

CoolKidFacts.com

DailyKos.com

Dailymail.co.uk

DataLounge.com

DidTrumpTweetIt.com

East Bay Times

eelp.law.harvard.edu

Elite Daily

FactCheck.org

FarmlandGrab.org

Financial Times

Forbes.com

ForeignPolicy.com

Fortune.com

Fox News

HedgeClippers.org

High Country News

HolocaustForgotten.com

Huffpost.com

Inc.com

Inquisitr.com

JewishInsider.com

JewishVirtualLibrary.org

KansasCity.com

MarketBeat.com

MarketWatch.com

MediaBiasFactCheck.com

Mediaite.com

MoneyMorning.com

Mother Jones

MSN.com

NationalFile.com

NationalMemo.com

NBC News

NeedToImpeach.com

News Channel 3

NewsMax.com

Newsweek.com

NYDailyNews.com

OpenHeartedRebellion.com

OpenSecrets.org

OurPublicService.org

Palmer Report

PBS.org

PlagiarismToday.com

Politico.com

PolitiFact.com

ProPublica

RawStory.com

ReverseMortgageDaily.com

RightWingWatch.org

Robert Reich – YouTube Channel

rtfitchauthor.com

Salon.com

SierraClub.org

Slate.com

TampaBay.com

TheAtlantic.com

The Conservative Investor Daily

TheDailyBeast.com

TheGuardian.com

TheIntercept.com

The New Republic

The New York Times

TheUptake.org

TheSportster.com

TheTablet.org

The Wall Street Journal

The Washington Post

TownandCountryMag.com

Travel and Leisure

TrumpGolfCount.com

Union of Concerned Scientists

USA Today

Vice.com

WashingtonExaminer.com

WashingtonMonthly.com

Wikipedia

WokeSloth.com

Wrestlinginc.com

Disclaimer:

Information in this book is based on previously published news reports from a wide variety of sources. The author took extreme care in researching and cross-referencing sources for this collection in order to ensure all information is as accurate as possible. But she is not a reporter. She has not personally verified any of the data in this book.

Whenever information about a person was not readily available in mainstream sources, the author marked the content as *possibly* being misleading.

Therefore, in an abundance of caution, the author does not represent the information contained herein as personally verified.

Further, the author does not profess to know anyone featured in this work directly. Though based on extensive research and the most likely probabilities, any mention of motives or personal thoughts is speculation on the author's part.

I hope you enjoyed this book and have gained some insights from the reading.

No doubt you will also appreciate –
<u>Shameless Svengali: 101 Questions Americans Need Trump to Answer HONESTLY!</u>

This is the first book I wrote about Trump and is also available on Amazon.

It would mean a lot to me if readers would write an online review. Even a few words can be incredibly insightful. Your thoughts are helpful to the author and potential readers as well!

Thank you so much!!

If you like freebies (and who doesn't?), join my mailing list. Send me an email – with YOUR NAME, and the word SUBSCRIBE in the subject to:

Karen@KarenAnnCarpenter.com

I'd love to hear from you!

You can also find me on Twitter: @KACAuthor